Corruption in Nigeria – The Niger Delta Experience

I0091026

Edited by
Christian Akani

FOURTH DIMENSION PUBLISHING CO., LTD.

First Published 2002 by
FOURTH DIMENSION PUBLISHING CO., LTD.
16 Fifth Ave, City Layout, P.M.B. 01164, Enugu, Nigeria
email: fdpbooks@aol.com, nwankwov@infoweb.abs.net
Web site: http://www.fdpbooks.com.

ISBN 978-156-485-7

CONDITIONS OF SALE

Design and Typesetting by
Fourth Dimension Publishers, Enugu

Contents

Preface

Nigeria has come a long way, but it is still saddled with many unfathomable socio-economic and political contradictions. These inhibit its match to development. These inhibitions are as brooding to the body politic, as they are noticeable in all aspect of the country's life.

The result is that instead of the country which was a beacon of hope for the black race in the 1960's to boldly enter into the path of modernity, it is gradually atrophying and shrinking to the cocoon of primitivity, destruction of self by self and completely unconcerned about the future of its people.

It is amazing that in the 21st century, corruption has become a mind-boggling phenomenon in the economic calculation of Nigerians. Few people manipulate their privileged position to dupe the country of billions of money meant for public use and go scot-free. The future portends danger if things continue to happen in this fatuous manner.

This work therefore, is humble contribution to salvage our country that is neckdeep in militant avarice and self-destructive greed. No country can expect a progressive future if its resources are unconscionably stolen by a few unproductive and unpatriotic people.

It is our hope that this book will serve as a trigger, a tonic to prick our conscience, to question hopelessness, halt the drift, the decadence and this culture of rabid accumulative instinct.

Dedication

This book is dedicated to Lady Judith Ashby

Notes on Contributors

Mr. Christian Akani is a seasoned human rights activist. He has written many books, and was Chairman of the Committee for the Defence of Human Rights, Rivers State Branch. He is presently the Executive Director, Institute of Academic Freedom in Nigeria.

Dr. Anam Ndu is the Director of Operation at the Professor Claude Ake Centre for Advanced Social Science. He has written many papers on the Niger Delta question.

Professor Esko Toyo is a Professor of Economics at the University of Calabar. He is a strong member of the Academic Staff Union of Nigerian Universities (ASU). He has written many books and is best known for his objectivity.

Dr. Arthur A. Nwankwo is one of the most prolific writers Africa has produced. He is the Chancellor of the Eastern Mandate Union and participated in pro-democracy struggles in the country. He has written many books on the Nigerian political development.

Acknowledgement

The production of this book is a collectivity of efforts of many people. It would be difficult to exhaust our depth of gratitude to them. Without their dogged commitment, advice and encouragement, this book would not have been possible.

First, we are grateful to all the resource persons who graciously accepted to present papers for this conference at great risk: Dr. Arthur Nwankwo, Professor Esko Toyo, and Dr. Anam Ndu.

We are also grateful to the participants whose contributions immensely beefed up the quality of the conference, particularly Dr. N.E. Bassey Duke and Mr. Paterson Ogon of Ijaw Council for Human Rights.

Finally, we are mostly indebted to Mr. Karl Uchegbu of Nigerian Institute of Human Rights, Mr. Steve Obodoekwe, Mr. Sunny Anya, Mr. Cletus Ugbana and Miss Queen Ugoji for all their contributions to the success of the conference.

Welcome Address

Welcome address by Akani Christian on the conference on Corruption in Nigeria: The Niger Delta Experience organized by the Institute of Academic Freedom in Nigeria (IAFN), in collaboration with USAID/OTI on 26th - 27th May, 2000 at Royal Garden Hotel, Rumuomasi Port Harcourt, Rivers State.

The Chairman,

Hon. Commissioner of Justice & Attorney General, Rivers State,

Chairman of A.N. Rivers State Chapter,

Respected Resource persons,

Ladies & Gentlemen.

On behalf of the Institute of Academic Freedom in Nigeria, (IAFN), I wish to warmly express our pride and profuse happiness for this gathering. This is important considering the integrity of the resource persons and the carefully chosen participants. It is indeed a memorable event and we are encouraged by this demonstration of unflinching solidarity.

IAFN is a non-governmental organization that emerged on 22nd March 1998. This was a time when our Universities had lost their autonomy and unscholarly ethics were introduced into the university system because of the tyrannical rule of Generals Ibrahim Babangida and Sani Abacha.

Its avowed aim included:

1. To highlight the conditions of Nigerian universities.
2. To create a virile enabling environment for learning and the pursuit of knowledge.
3. To engage in debates, workshops, and seminars that would enhance the quality of learning and research.

The Institute is ardently committed to gender equality, academic freedom, and good governance. It has published many books and has a quarterly journal called the *Academic*. The theme of today's conference "Corruption in Nigeria: the Niger Delta Experience," is not only apt but timely. It is on record that the virus of corruption has done a lot of damage to our democratic experiment. Public officers more often regard their offices as gold mines and God-sent opportunities, to flagrantly loot and amass wealth.

They display this looted wealth in an annoying and obscene manner that glorifies corruption as something worthy to operate. The result is a cyclical dance of polluted and corrupt-ridden life style which has reduced our attempts to develop to futility.

It was against this background that we have painstakingly selected the specialists to examine this phenomenon and proffer sustainable solutions. We are also aware that corruption is directly linked with the country's dependent, colonized and unplanned capitalist mode of production, an economy supported with a single commodity and seriously manipulated by the global capitalist system.

Our claim to democracy would be a mirage if the legacies of corruption are not permanently cleaned up. We, therefore, call on the Federal Government of Nigeria to urgently invoke the relevant statutes so that all public officers who corruptly enriched themselves would be punished.

In other to carry out this campaign beyond this place, we intend to publish the proceedings of this Conference for public consumption.

IAFN is grateful to members of the Advisory Board, our admirers and the press for their concern and support. We owe a debt of gratitude to USAID/OTI for their wonderful support. Without them, this conference would not have taken place.

We hope that if we invite you next time you will come.

Thank you.

Akani Christian
Executive Director.

The Institute

The Institute of Academic Freedom In Nigeria (IAFN) emerged on March 22, 1998 against the background of institutional decay, low academic standard and suppression of knowledge.

The Institute arose as part of the efforts to strengthen the country's democratic experiment and uphold the virtues of criticality. This is because there can be no democracy without an enlightened mass. Its motto is 'Education is a right to all humans.'

Its avowed objective includes:
1. To highlight the conditions of Nigerian Universities.
2. To create a virile enabling environment for learning and the pursuit of knowledge.
3. To engage in debates, workshops and seminars that would enhance the quality of learning and research.

Some of its major activities are;
1. The Academic - A quarterly journal of the Institute.
2. IAFN Lecture.
3. Esther Sister Akani Memorial Lecture and Scholarship Award for girls in tertiary institutions.

For more information contact:
The Executive Director
Institute of Academic Freedom In Nigeria (IAFN)
P.O. Box 455
University of Port Harcourt
Choba, Port Harcourt,
Rivers State, Nigeria.
email: iafn@yahoo.com.

Communique of the IAFN Conference on "Corruption in Nigeria: The Niger Delta Experience"

Preamble

A two-day conference organised by the Institute for Academic Freedom in Nigerian on "Corruption in Nigeria: The Niger Delta Experience" was attended by representatives of Civil Society (NGOs and CBOs), Government agencies, ethnic nationality groups, and the mass media. Presentations and comments by participants and resource persons agreed that corruption, like instability is a major recurrent issue of governance in Nigeria, particularly in the Niger Delta. This is because of its pervasiveness, scale and sophistication. Therefore, an understanding of the phenomenon of corruption in the Niger Delta nay, Nigeria must be situated within the context of the character of the Nigerian State.

These positions were based on the following observations:

1. That the issue of corruption in Nigeria is part of the crises of the Nigerian State.
2. That the Nigerian State is a colonial creation, controlled by a coterie of men who are endemically individualistic, with a tenuous productive base, but lavishly ostentatious.

   - There is the necessity of renegotiating the terms of the Federal Union including a new fiscal federalism that is based on local ownership and control of resources reminiscent of the regional days.

   - To curb the propensity of corruption, the Nigerian State must be free from private manipulation. It must be above selfish and sectional considerations.

   - The ideals of democracy and rule of law must flourish. All those who corruptly enriched themselves must necessarily face the law.

   - There should be an immediate end to the peripheral, dependent and oil and gas mono-economy as it is practised in Nigeria. The economy should be sectorally diversified with emphasis on production rather than consumption and exchange.

- Government should embark on a programme of anti-corruption crusade. Strict family values, moral instruction, transparency in governance and accountability should form the fulcrum of this crusade. The mass media, schools, orientation agencies and other agents of socialisation should be involved in this campaign.

- Employment and appointments should be based on merit.

- Monetary settlement of community members by oil trans-national companies in form of sit-at-home allowance, and public relations should be discouraged. Gainful employment and life-sustaining projects and amenities should be seriously encouraged.

Summary Report

The Conference commenced by 10.30 a.m. with a brief opening remarks by Dr. Ntete Duke who chaired the session. Dr. Duke remarked that corruption in Nigeria had reached a crisis stage. This had generated enough public revulsion and condemnation from anti-corruption crusaders.

He also emphasised that we have to make a distinction between genuine crusaders and the so-called "corrective" regimes. While the former is really intent on removing past abuses and placing the system on a path of rectitude, the latter may be an apologia for predatory or oligarchic leadership.

In his welcome address Mr. Christian Akani the Executive Director of the Institute for Academic Freedom In Nigeria (IAFN) lamented the upsurge of corrupt practices among Nigerians. He noted that corruption had eaten deep into our marrows. The people, he said should form the pivot of anti-corruption campaigns. He commended USAID/OTI for facilitating the grant which made the conference possible. He declared that with such partners like USAID/OTI, the process of eliminating negative vices like corruption in Nigeria has not only begun, but would be realised in the fullness of time.

Political Economy of Corruption in Nigeria

In this presentation Dr. Arthur Nwankwo, Chancellor, Eastern Mandate Union (EMU) and National Vice Chairman, NADECO, posited that corruption in Nigeria had become endemic and eaten deep into the fabric of the nation. Institutions of government have become medium for theft and corruption.

He identified several approaches to explaining corruption. These included the Western liberal approach, the Marxist approach, the Moral approach and the Revisionist approach.

In discussing forms of corruption, he noted that the most corrupt sector in Nigeria is the Petroleum Industry. Corruption got to its crescendo under the military, hence they are responsible for the decay. Every regime brought its own form of corruption. Gen. Gowon's regime was a Father Christmas, spending questionable billions of naira on empty projects, activities and neighbouring countries.

Under the regimes of Alhaji Shehu Shagari, Major Generals Buhari, Babangida and the draconian Abacha Junta, Nigeria transcended the threshold of corruption to blatant stealing. These regimes perpetrated economic genocide against millions of Nigerians. He noted that in Nigeria today, the common wealth is being shared like spoils of war.

Dr. Nwankwo articulated the following solutions to corruption in Nigeria;

a. Nigeria should go back to the practice of true Federalism. This, he said, will be achieved by restructuring of the polity.

b. Convening of a Sovereign National Conference (SNC) to, among others, thrash out issues of control of resources by ethnic nationalities.

c. Rejection of the 1999 Constitution because it is incapable of fighting corruption as it is replete with objectionable clauses.

Nigerian state as an instrument of corruption

Christian Akani, a scholar of Political Theory examined the extent the State had helped to consolidate corruption. He noted that in Nigeria the State does not see itself as an impartial umpire of the people. He discovered five characteristics of the Nigerian state: *Viz*

1) the State emerged after long years of colonialism;
2) it is subservient and dependent on the global capitalist system;
3) it does not produce anything but depends solely on consumption;
4) the economy is dominantly controlled by the petty bourgeoisie in collaboration with TNCs;
5) it is a rentier state that collects rents and royalties mainly in the oil sector.

Mr. Akani asserted that the aim of capitalist mode of production is profit. To achieve this goal, all obstacles are crushed. This, in itself is a manifestation of corruption as it encourages negative practices. He warned that it would be very difficult for the state to campaign against corruption because it is corruption personified. Politicians and controllers of state power take politics to mean wealth, influence and affluence. The Nigerian State is part of the problem, instead of being the agent for solving the problem.

He concluded by noting that corruption is not a natural component of man but is a historical consequence.

Corruption and the Challenges of Development In the Niger Delta

In this paper Dr. Ekang Anam-Ndu, Director of Operations at the Centre for Advanced Social Science, Port Harcourt, argued that corruption in the Niger Delta must be situated within the character of the Nigerian State. He noted that corruption like instability is a major recurrent issue of governance in Nigeria especially the Niger Delta. He pointed out that the political elite in the Niger Delta would be examined in an attempt to understand the problem. Corruption, he said, inhibits development. It is an instrument of internal colonisation and underdevelopment.

He posited that the crisis of corruption in Nigeria is part of the Nigerian State. It can hardly be solved without addressing the crisis of the Nigerian State. "It appears to me that we have to accept the necessity of renegotiating the terms of the Federal Union including a new fiscal federalism that is based on local ownership and control of resources reminiscent of the regional days".

In terms of fighting corruption, it is clear that much cannot and will not be achieved given the timid way the problem is approached and the embarrassingly shameful trend in our political engineering in which ex-public officials known to have ruined our treasury for years are now deified.

The Non-Centrality of Corruption - Theses

Prof. Eskor Toyo, Social Thinker and Professor of Economics, University of Calabar said that corruption had affected the whole world not just Nigeria.

He exhorted participants to be careful concerning Marxism since many things said about Marx are distortions. He agrees with postulations made in other papers pointing out that corruption should be fought through mass mobilisation. He said that mass action also needs a conscious leadership.

He also warned against polarising or ethnicising the problem as North vs South, Ibo vs Yoruba; observing that the peasants in the North are worse off than those in the south. He drew attention to the historical farce that the Nigerian/Biafran war was the first civil war in Nigeria, noting than the first civil war was started by the Tivs in 1960 and 1964. They were massacred in their thousands in what has been disparagingly named as the Tiv uprising.

Prof. Eskor Toyo described capitalism as modern slavery while noting that Nigeria does not fall into the definition of modern society. He declared that what we practice in Nigeria is plutocracy as opposed to democracy. He pointed out that in capitalist societies, evidence of corruption are contained in laws, accounting rules, social systems, religion etc. He opined that capitalism exploits people through the following ways;

1. exploitation of the wage system;
2. exploitation of the consumer;
3. exploitation of the State;
4. exploitation by the use of State power.

This, he said, had bred such corrupt practices as the spoils system ie; rewarding party supporters with jobs, contracts etc. Through the lobby system, capitalism has left in its wake unbridled philistinism. Most times tribalism is often used to cover up corruption.

Militarism and Corruption

Mr. Nelson Azibolanari, environmental activist and Geography teacher at the University of Port Harcourt, started his presentation by saying that he plans to make it as participatory as possible. He drew attention to the way soldiers corrupted the Niger Delta.

His presentation was made up of five parts; *viz* military and corruption, instances of corruption, effects and solutions. In examining the link between military and corruption, he opined that the mere act of military coup is itself an act of corruption. He also stated that all military coups are motivated by the urge to share the wealth of the nation. He maintained that such military policies and legislations as the Land Use Decree Act of 1978, Gas Flaring and Associated Gas Re-injection Decree, OMPADEC and NDDC 2000 are indeed corrupt as they are mainly the drain pipes of the rulers.

The Military in power has colluded with the oil multinationals to unleash on the people and their environment acts of "ECO-vandalism" and environmental degradation.

Hc was of the view that in its greed to wealth and accumulate social surplus, the military had supervised human rights violations, extra-judicial killings and wholesale extermination campaigns as has been witnessed in Umuechem Ogoni 1995, Iko, Choba 2000, Odi 2000, Oleh and Bakolori 1982. The unbridled accumulation of the social surplus has also led to intra and inter-communal clashes and ethnic rivalries.

Group work and discussions

In the discussion session that followed the presentations, participants focused on the theme, 'Corruption In Nigeria: the Niger Delta Experience.' They reviewed among other things, the nature and structure of the modern Nigerian State *vis-à-vis* corruption.

Mr. Patterson Ogon, Executive Director, Ijaw Council for Human Rights (ICHR), observed that no mention was made of Obasanjo's government and also noted that nothing was said about the anti-corruption bill which he said had continued to lie in the dustbin of the National Assembly. Mr. Wisedom Dike, Executive Director, Community Rights Initiative (CORI) remarked that it was phony that Obasanjo refused to sign the anti-corruption bill because the immunity for the executive branch and its officers was removed. On the issue of 13% derivation, Dike said that it was fraudulent and annoying. He said that Obasanjo removed N200 billion accumulated arrears from the 13% derivation. So what is Obasanjo up to, he queried? As if that was not enough, Obasanjo had reintroduced the offshore – onshore dichotomy. Mr. Dike summed up by saying that 13% derivation meant 87% deprivation.

Nelson Azibolanari, Geography lecturer, University of Port Harcourt said he waited to hear the peculiar scenario created by the Nigerian State. How come the Nigerian State is peculiar to corruption? To buttress his points, he stated that in Nigeria, people who took public funds are rewarded with national honours and chieftaincy titles. He also stated that corruption in Nigeria is pervasive because the money that is being stolen is also in the first place stolen money from oil communities of the Niger Delta. He suggested that fighting corruption will require popular action.

Ruskin Amadi, correspondent with Community News, noted that though most of the presentations were good, there was a vacuum, most failed to proffer solutions. He then asked if we should allow the state to provide solutions, since the state itself is a key actor, or should solution come by way of mass popular action as suggested by Mr. Azibolanari.

Mr. Wisedom Dike, commenting on the way forward noted that the community owns the resources being looted. Quoting Article 20 of the African Charter, he called for a conscious effort by the people to stop the looting of resources. He called for mass action and organisation of communities.

Sylvia Obene, representing the International Federation of Women Lawyers (FIDA) wanted to know the make up of Niger Delta, was it the six states that make up the geo-political south-south or the states mentioned as beneficiaries of NDDC?

Arguing along the same line Ruskin Amadi of Community News opined that the problem with Nigeria is the issue of power relations and domination among the ethnic groups. He asked if with the unfolding scenarios in the middle belt and attempts to re-declare Biafra, the end was not in sight for Nigeria?

Wisedom Dike observed that so much money is being pumped into the local governments in the Niger Delta, yet there is nothing to show for it. He queried: Should we continue to wait until the nation state is dismantled before we commit ourselves to developing our society?

Gold Rebuben of Community Rights Initiative commenting on gas flaring wanted to know if it was right to tax the oil multinationals for flaring gas. This was because of its deleterious effect on the environment and if any group was doing anything to combat gas flaring or are we to allow the gas to be flared eternally?

Emeni J. Okon, Secretary, Women in Nigeria (WIN) Rivers State branch, shared an experience she had with other participants. She said that on April, 22 which was marked worldwide as Earthday, she was part of a team that visited some communities in the Niger Delta. At Obite, a major oil and gas centre, the team was confronted by the sight of rusted, dilapidated pipes used in transporting crude oil, cris-crossing a primary school. She noted that the primary school was without chairs, desks and other utilities. Both in front and behind the school lay pipelines carrying billions of dollars worth of crude oil. She said that time for keeping quiet was over. She wondered how the children were learning in such an environment and what their fate would be in the event of a blow out or a rupture in the pipes. Reacting to some of the issues raised, Mr. Paterson Ogon informed participants that the government and the oil multinationals had variously said that they would end gas flaring by 2008 which he said was too far.

Mr. Ukaegbu Karl Chinedu, Resident Researcher with the Centre for Peace and Conflict Studies of the Nigeria Institute of Human Rights (NIHR) commended Mr. Azibolanari for not restricting his presentation to the Weberian and Marxian theories of the state, but for locating the critical mass of his presentation within the context of the historical experience of the Niger Delta people. Mr. Uchegbu posited that the worst form of corruption in the Niger Delta is the corruption of power itself. He noted that under successive regimes especially that of Babangida and Abacha, the State was privatised. The Military adopted informal repression as a directive principle of state policy. Thus the Military created centres of instability to remain glued to power while fanning the embers of inter-communal, and inter-ethnic strife. He noted that today the Niger Delta region remains the most militarised with attendant consequences for the people.

Mr. Napoleon Ewoh, a labour veteran said that groups like IAFN, USAID/OTI should ensure that the campaign against corruption should not end in conference halls. He said that the campaign should be taken to rural communities as a way of mobilising the people to fight corruption. Nimi David – West of Institute of Academic Freedom In Nigeria in her contribution said that we should start the fight against corruption in our homes and families because the family unit is a very important arm of society.

Working group discussions and recommendations

After the presentations and the session for questions and comments, the conference broke into two working groups which discussed the issues raised in the presentations. The groups also made their recommendations and suggested that future action should be undertaken.

Acts of corrupt practices and those involved

Group I: They identified the following acts of corrupt practices and those involved.

a. Embezzlement: Contractors, Traditional Leaders, Local Government Chairmen, Office Holders (Public and Private) Youth leaders, Military Officers.

b. Misapplication of Funds: Politicians, Local Government Chairmen, Church Leaders, Multinational Oil Companies.

c. Lack of Accountability: Non–Governmental Organisations, Government Ministries and Parastatals, Community Leaders, Church Leaders.

d. Extortion: Police Officer, Custom Officers, Revenue Officials, Civil Servants, Lecturers.

e. Favouring School authorities, Government Ministries/Parastatals, Politicians/Political Office Holders, Families.

f. Obtaining by False Pretences: Policemen, Contractors, Businessmen, Youth Leaders, Church Leaders

g. Rigging: Politicians, Students, Lecturers, Electoral Officers, Politicians, Government Officials.

h. Professional Misconduct: Journalists, Lawyers, Doctors, Accountants.

i. Over-Invoicing: Contractors, Politicians, Businessmen/Women, Non-Governmental Organisations, Accountants.

j. Adulteration: Traders, Producers/Manufacturers, Lecturers.

Classification of Corruption

    A. Petty class Corruption:
- Cheating.
- Examination Malpractice.
- Stealing.

- Lying.
- Bribery in the Civil Service.

B. Middle Class Corruption.
- Bribing of Traditional Rulers by oil companies.
- Lack of Transparency among NGOs.
- Favouritism.
- Swindling by False Revenue Agents in Collusion with Local Government chairmen.
- Diversion of Community Funds by community.
- Development Committee (CDC) Members.

C. High Level Corruption:
- Misappropriation of Funds by Public officers.
- Poor Execution of Contracts by contractors in Collusion with Government Officials.
- Misapplication of funds by Public Officers.
- Stealing of Public Property by Public Officers.
- Bribing of Public Officials by Oil Companies to lower Standards.

Recommendations

1. IAFN should develop a strategy for reaching out to people in the grassroots with the anti-corruption message.
2. IAFN should assist students and lecturers in the Universities to resist corruption without being victimised.
3. Codes of conduct should be drawn up for NGOs to root out corrupt practices among NGO Leaders.
4. USAID/OTI to support Coalitions and Networks working to eradicate corruption as well as build the capacities of grassroot organisations *viz* strategic planning, advocacy and campaigns etc., to make the war against corruption winnable.
5. IAFN should address the issues of corruption, sexual harassment and human rights abuses in Universities, Polytechnics and Colleges of Education in the Niger Delta.
6. Development/Strengthening procedures which ensure that misappropriation of funds are checkmated.
7. Support processes ensuring that oil companies stop paying monetary inducement to chiefs, youths and oil bearing communities.
8. IAFN to facilitate the setting up of a coalition of Niger Delta NGOs working in the area of corruption to serve as a

watch-dog on public spendings and also to train a crop of anti-corruption crusaders. Such coalition to be known as NGO Coalition against Corruption (NGO-CAC).

9. IAFN to facilitate setting up of Anti-Corruption Brigades (ACB) at the grassroot level to train local people on how to develop a culture of resistance to bribery and corruption.

10. Prison sentences shall be mandatory for all those found guilty of corruption.

11. All laws conferring on public officials immunity to accountability must be repealed.

12. Freedom of the press must be upheld. This means among other things that media practitioners must not be intimidated or harassed in any way in the lawful performance of their duties.

Conclusions

This Conference recognises the opportunity presented by Nigeria's return to democracy and the political space which has opened up, setting the country on a new path towards justice, equity and democracy. It is also aware of the fragility of the process of changes that have begun and the many obstacles to progress which are yet to be addressed. In this regard all civil society actors and Nigerians should recognise that appropriate action over the next one year will be crucial – time is short if the present democratic experiment will not be short-lived.

This is illustrated by the "business – as – usual" manner in which the Obasanjo administration has in one year in office tried to beat the looting record of the Abacha evil empire. The legislators' furniture allowance and the whooping ₦22 billion which the legislators earmarked for themselves offers a peek into the Aso Rock mind set.[*] The effect is that the Anti-Corruption Bill has been rendered obsolete on arrival.

---

[*] The accusations and counter accusations of corrupt leadership which has degenerated to frequent leadership change in the National Assembly and the obscene flamboyance of controllers of State power vividly point to the fact that corruption has been institutionalised in our socio-political marrows.

Chapter One

Overview

Akani Christian

Corruption the world over is a condemnable phenomenon. But to those who practise it, it confers some benefits. The majority groan under its triumph. Essentially, it is often used as a mechanism for political accumulation and private appropriation of wealth.

In whatever way, corruption is a wasting disease and generally defined as 'the abuse of public position for private or sectional gain - flourishes most where politcians and officials exercise power without accountability'.

It is important to note that the moment man left the "state of nature", and aggressively subdued his environment to his whims, such vices like avarice, greed and corruption were gradually introduced into the society. These vices also exposed their inherent changes and contradictions in the society.

> Corruption, therefore, does not have divine origin but a reflection of historical integration of man and his environment in the production and reproduction of goods and services.[1]

Ekekwe has argued that corruption is part and parcel of the economic culture of capitalism, doggedly hinged on possessive individualism. It is the organic unit that accelerates the locomotion of predatory mode of production.

The whole process of slavery, imperialism and colonial subjugation and bastardization of pre-colonial setting was a graphic presentation of corruption for accumulation of wealth. In other words, the main goal of corruption is the satisfaction of a private objective to the neglect of the majority.

This was why the continent of Africa was mercilessly ravaged without redress and stereotyped as an inferior specimen of humanity. Draconian and extremely repressive systems such

---

[1] Akani Christian, 'Anti-corruption, Transparency and accountability in Nigeria' Paper Presented at a three day workshop on "Conflict Mitigation and Good Governance" Organized by the Partners for Peace, Advocacy and Good Governance (PAPAGG) 8 -10 November, 2001 at Nike Lake Hotel, Enugu State p. 2.

as apartheid and assimilation policy were used to enhance the corruption of the place and quicken surplus appropriation. According to the philosophical radicals, colonization was seen as an outlet for the country's (Britain) surplus capital. This is why V.I. Lenin noted that:

> It is common knowledge that colonies are conquered with fire and sword, that the population of the colonies are brutally treated and that they are exploited in a thousand ways (by exporting capital through concessions, etc cheating in the sale of goods, submission to the authorities of the 'ruling nation', and so on...)[2]

Unfortunately, the emergence of Africa into the world division of labour as a politically sovereign continent did not help matters. The continent not only imbibed the ethos, values and predatory disposition of capitalism, but fell into the hands of a gang who nearly perfected the looting spree and corrupt tendencies of the colonialists. These people scattered in different countries of Africa have perpetuated more woes and pain on their countrymen than any other group as in Mobutu's Zaire (Congo) General Sani Abacha's Nigeria and Samuel Doe's Liberia to mention a few. Mobutu and Sani Abacha through their Kleptomanic activities emerged as 'world champion swindlers'. According to Naidoo:

Through repression Mobutu systematically plundered the economy, destroyed all economic and social infrastructure and reduced the Congolese people to abject poverty.[3]

Naidoo went on to say that, the emergence of President Laurent Kabila further privatized the Congolese economy saddled with more than $300m debt owned to the IMF and World Bank. The keys to the 'upper chamber' where the country's safe is located in the "Marble Palace" in Kinshasa is constantly in Kabila's pocket.[4]

The situation is not different in Ghana, Zimbabwe, and Malawi. 'Nozim' responsible for the procurement and

---

[2] V. I Lenin, *On Imperialism and Imperialists*, (Moscow: Progress Publishers, 1977) p. 39.

[3] South African Year Book of International Affairs 1999/2000 p. 328.

[4] Ibid p. 322.

distribution of fuel in the country was seen as the 'most corrupt'. This may have motivated a High Court Judge to suggest the need to come up with a concrete action plan on how to tackle corruption and develop a code of ethics[5]. In Malawi, the era of Hastings Amuzu Banda can be likened to that of Abacha, Ibrahim Babangida and Mobutu. Banda not only stashed billions of dollars away in Swiss and London Banks, but attempts to recover this money through the Malawi and British courts failed.[6]

It is most important to note that transnational companies through their grand manoeuvers, oil the organic existence of corruption. These are in form of 'success fees' and kick back's. The result is that there is a cyclical movement of corruption which benefits a few but gradually ruins the economy. The report of the South Commission states that Corruption gradually ruins the economy, that 'corruption has been on the increase in many countries in all parts of the world'....

It is...

> the enemy of progress, but corrupt leaders cling to power, opposing efforts to open government curbing personal freedoms and abusing basic human rights, that corruption crushes that potential benefits of free market forces. The businessman goes broke, the rules of a healthy economic system becomes twisted, and companies addicted to paying bribes become rotten. In consequence, prospects for economic progress, so vital to social development are ruined.[7]

We can discern three negative consequences of corruption on a country.

1. The state becomes dictatorial and violent.
2. Poverty and agony become the lot of the majority.
3. The above may harden and degenerate into civil disobedience and raw violence which Anam Ndu highlighted in his paper.

Nigeria has experienced the above effects. Achebe stated that corruption has reached the alarming stage and entered the

---

[5] *Business Africa*, June 1999 p. 24.
[6] Ibid p. 30
[7] Dr. Gabriel Okara, Nigeria Prometheus Bound p. 8.

fatal and critical stages and that Nigeria will die if we keep pretending that she is only slightly indisposed.[8] Ake also warned that as 'a society of beggars, parasites and bandits' Nigeria 'cannot know peace or stability, and it cannot be democratic in the real sense. It can only gravitate endlessly as we are doing presently in material poverty and moral regression[9].

This is why all our political and democratic experiments have been flawed by unprecedented violence and high-level brigandage since the country got independence. While about six Nigerians are among the richest in the world, such as chief Harry Akande occupying the seventh position ($533m monthly income), Chief Akindele Fernandez nineteenth position, ($469m monthly income) General Ibrahim Babangida Seventy-Sixth position ($216m monthly income), and Chief Arthur Nzeribe Ninety-sixth position ($162m monthly income); members of the billionaire club included Mrs. Maryam Babangida, Chief Philip Asiodu, Alhaji Umaru Dikko. Dr Joseph Wayas, Admiral Augustus Aikhomu (rtd) and Mallam Ali Makele.[10] The poverty line in the country is widely expanding. The country is saddled with an army of unemployed youths whose incessant restiveness had led to the development of unethical conducts, a $30b debt, infant mortality rate per 1,000 live births and GNP per capita $280. The above is a graphic representation of crushing poverty in the midst of stinking affluence by a few. These are the cost a country has to bear for allowing corruption to penetrate its life-marrow.

Esko Toyo was right when he stated that 'like other forms of exploitation, corruption is one way of privately appropriating the social surplus'.

Like in other African countries that are committed to the elimination of corruption, the Chief Olusegun Obasanjo administration has enacted the Anti-Corruption Act of 2000. It stated that;

---

[8] Dr. Arthur Nwankwo, *Political Economy of Corruption in Nigeria*. Paper presented at a two day Seminar organised by the Institute of Academic Freedom in Nigeria (IAFN) at Royal Garden Hotel Port, Harcourt 26 - 27th May, 2000 p. 2.

[9] Ibid p. 13.

[10] *The Punch* Newspaper, December 20, 2000.

Any person who asks for, receives or obtains any benefit before doing his or her duty is liable to imprisonment for seven years, fraudulent acquisition of property shall on conviction be liable to seven years imprisonment, any person who corruptly gives or procures any property or benefit to a police officer for another person shall be liable on conviction to seven years imprisonment.[11]

The above example has been replicated in other countries like the Zambian Anti-Corruption Commission (1980), Malawian Anti-Corruption Bureau and the Corruption Practices Act. Infact, the 'World bank is actually planning to fund research to determine 'scientifically' the extent of corruption in Malawi'.

Corruption should be condemned and de-emphasized in all ramifications especially at this stage of our democratic experiment. This book is therefore appropriate for it would contribute to the corpus of literature that would enhance the cultivation of 'anti-fraud culture, promote a clear anti-fraud policy, and programmes that would thoroughly and completely wipe out avarice, greed, corruption and covetousness in our body politic.

This is a clarion call for a total overhaul of the country's economic foundation, distributive system, leadership disposition and relationship to public wealth and property.

Ndu noted that corruption grew rapidly in the country because;

the reason for this is to be sought not in the complex socio-political milieu called Nigeria as has been claimed, but in the fraudulent leadership contraption which Nigeria has always had and which is always a crisis phenomenon.[12]

Nigerians should rethink, evaluate their lifestyles, values and standards. They should begin to jettison militant materialism, cheating to gain undue advantage at whatever levels. They should begin to appreciate that corruption is a crime against humanity and the unborn generation, it grinds a state, country and community to a halt. They should begin to

---

[11] *Tell* Magazine, November, 20, 2000.
[12] Akani Christian, *Op Cit* p. 3.

conceptualize corruption as a '... theft from the nation, and theft from the nation is always theft from the weakest in the nation, the old, the disabled, the sick, the children and the new born'.[13]

This is the vision of IAFN.

Akani Christian
Mgbuoba Rumuokwuta
31 December, 2000

---

[13] *Business Africa Op Cit* p. 19.

Chapter Two

Political Economy of Corruption in Nigeria

Dr Arthur Agwuncha Nwankwo[*]

Let me state without mincing words that I am happy to be in your midst today to rub minds on the one grave problem we have all come to regard as an intractable problem. I am indeed glad to be associated with this conference since it will afford us the opportunity to exhaustively discuss the political economy of corruption in Nigeria. I congratulate the organizers for their foresight and commitment to the high ideals of transparency, probity, and accountability, which will ultimately lead to the birth of a great nation.

This conference could not have come at a more auspicious time - a period the present government is waging intensive war against corruption. Our contributions today would go a long way to pointing the way forward in our resolve to rid our society of corruption.

The paper you have saddled me with is by no means an easy task to say the least. I accepted to present the paper for the simple reason that it is an area I consider very relevant if there must be a tomorrow for our generation and those yet unborn. There are other reasons for which I accepted to do the paper. The first reason is that the paper will help us focus attention on those anatomy and situational indices, which exacerbate corruption in Nigeria. Secondly, a society conceived and born in corruption cannot but breed suffocating decay. This is essentially true of our society as evidenced in the high-tech nature of corruption.

The forgoing will help us to locate the analytical frame work of this paper, to wit, that corruption in Nigeria is traceable to a number of factors notably the structural deficiencies of our society which have worked antithetically to our survival as a people. Prior to the creation of Nigeria, the various ethnic nationalities that today make up Nigeria have in-

---

[*] Chancellor, Eastern Mandate Union (EMU), National Vice-Chairman, National Democratic Coalition (NADECO).

built mechanisms for curbing corrupt practices. However, the establishment of Nigeria as a geo-political entity heightened inter-ethnic rivalry, which led to the intensification of the struggle for the control of the nation's resources among the various ethnic formations. We will equally look at such variables as revenue allocation, derivation principle, resource explanation, proper restructuring etc, as variables, which if properly employed could help stem the tide of corruption in Nigeria. You will now agree with me that the scope of our discussion is quite wide and required painstaking analysis. But the basic fact remains that corruption in Nigeria has assumed pandemic proportions. Society's gullibility and hallucinatory obsession for materialism led to perversion of our core values and created a semblance of acceptance of corruption.

This tragic reality has exerted negative impact on society with devastating consequences. The distortions and systematic destruction of the fabric of our society portends grave dangers not only to our nationhood but also existence. This seminar, I am glad to state, is a patriotic response to rescue a nation on the last lap of her dreaded descent to destruction.

Political Economy of Corruption In Nigeria

For a proper elucidation of our subject matter, it is necessary that we look at the meaning and scope of political economy. A discussion on the political economy of any society is the study of the polity. The basic character of any society is primarily determined by the economic super-structure. This is particularly so because it is the economic structure that provided the basic matrix upon which other structures are developed.

Political economy as a study of the socio-political dynamics of society, and as will be elucidated in the course of this paper will examine corruption in Nigeria. A good knowledge of the Nigerian society and character of its economy will help us understand the monstrosity of corruption.

In any society, public enterprises are generally recognized as instruments for rapid economic development of that society. Specifically, these enterprises are established to achieve the dual purpose of taking profits and achieving other societal objectives such as creating employment, eliminating or reducing mass poverty. Despite these expectations, state enterprises in developing countries like Nigeria have constantly sent out danger signals of inefficiency, official corruption and poor maintenance culture. Consequently public and private sectors in Nigeria have not been able to accomplish the noble objectives for which they were established. Rather, these institutions have become vehicles for profligacy, thievery and corruption.

For a deep insight, we shall look at two broad theoretical frameworks that have often been canvassed to account for the phenomenon of corruption - the Western Liberal perspective and the Marxist perspective.

The Western Liberal Perspective

Two schools or approaches are discernible with the Western Liberal Perspective. These are the Moralist Approach and the Revisionist Approach. The most popular approach to the explanation of corruption is the Moralist or Ethical one which attributes corruption to moral laxity or decadence; lack of common standard of morality, growing cultural and religious decay. The implication of this explanation of corruption is that if every citizen can be transformed into a religious and cultural fanatic, thus pre-colonial societies did not encourage individualistic or materialistic tendencies and corruption.

The Marxist Perspective

The Marxists provide an alternative theoretical framework to the explanation of corruption. According to them, the roots of corruption should not be sought in the values and attitudes of individuals in society, in other words, in the assumed nature of man, nor explained away simply as part and parcel of the social norms, values and practices of developing countries. Rather it should be sought in the nature of the social system.

Implicit in the Marxian perspective is that corruption is determined primarily by the prevalent social relations of production which itself can be explained by the mode of production. Kwanashi in 1983 had vigorously argued that the character and intensity of corruption is determined by the dominant mode of production and the associated social relations of production. Capitalist ideology has placed in the centre the private accumulation of wealth as the highest form of human activity. Corruption has thus become a very essential element of human activity in capitalist systems.

The Marxists, therefore, dismissed as very superficial, the Western Liberal explanation of corruption. They argue that underlying the moralist principle is a solid economic current. Corruption is not simply a moral issue, it is essentially a structural problem which derives from and has its existence in the soico-political and economic organization of society. As S.A. Nkom (1982) puts it, "... the belief that corruption emanates from bankrupt and redundant social values (whether modern or traditional) has mistaken the headache for fever because a society's social and moral values reflect and are firmly achored on specific material conditions. These material conditions are not determined by the ideas in people's heads but by the way society organizes the production, distribution and exchange of goods and services."

In this paper, I shall adopt the Marxist Approach in discussing the political economy of corruption in Nigeria. The rampant cases of corruption in Nigeria, is not just an issue of ethics or morality. It should be seen instead, as resulting from the peculiar nature of the state's social system. In other words, the neo-colonial and dependent capitalist nature of the Nigerian state has made it, and its apparatuses serve as vehicles for mindless corruption and primitive accumulation of wealth. It is this role of the neo-colonial state, says E. Ekekwe (1986) that distinguishes it from other states in the advanced capitalist countries.

In Nigeria, our social system has proved beyond question its ability to serve as instrument for building what Roger Murray (1977) defined as "administrative supported capitalism." The consequence is that both public and private institutions have constituted themselves as instruments that allow certain people in Nigeria to appropriate public money without recourse to probity and accountability. The diversion of public money into private pockets, is not a recent development in Nigeria. The Nigerian socio-political landscape brims with stories of scandals and squandering of our wealth by those in authority. Shortly after independence, following allegations of official high-handedness and financial mismanagement in Western Nigeria, the Government set up the Justice Coker Commission of Inquiry into the management of certain public corporations in the region. The Commission revealed that public funds were diverted into financing the Action Group through a company belonging to four top members of the party. Subsequent events revealed that the use of state machinery to facilitate private accumulation has become even more blatant and scandalous. Thus a critical look at the evolution of the Nigerian political culture cannot be complete without an exhaustive discourse on the origin and root of corruption in Nigeria. This can be related to the concepts of two publics where the private realm connotes the primordial public and the public realm connotes the civil structures/public *viz;* military, police, customs and excise and the civil service which also include the private sector. The outstanding characteristic is that the same political actors operate in the primordial and civic public. The Nigerian bourgeoisie was pervaded by a sense of insecurity as a result of ideological barrenness. The colonial state and imperial policies were primed to achieve a predictable subterfuge to influence their views and prejudices.

A great deal of anti-colonial activities by the Nigerian bourgeoisie consisted of encouragement to their followers to be late to work and to go on strikes for a variety of reasons. This situation created a marketable attitude to the extent that a Nigerian who evaded his tax was a hero, the Nigerian labourer who beat up his white employer was given extensive coverage in newspapers. In general, the Nigerian bourgeoisie class encouraged the common man to shirk his duties to the colonial government or else to define them as burdens. In the same breadth he encouraged him to demand for his rights. This attitude was a necessary sabotage against the white colonial government whom the Nigerian bourgeoisie class wanted to replace. This situation culminated into what I can describe as the "transfer effect" from colonialism to post colonial politics, in which there was demand for rights in excess of the available resources.

This generated a situation where the individual sees his public position as a moral obligation ordained by providence where he must steal by hook or by crook to sustain a primordial public of which he is a member. The existence of many ethnic groups in Nigeria equally bred a situation of rather tradition of informal taxation in the form of "voluntary" contribution to ethnic associations and other types of obligations to help with material gifts to the primordial public i.e. his community and place of birth, he, in turn receives from the primordial realm, benefits that are not materials but tangible in the form of identity or psychological security and or protection where the law catches up with the culprit.

The disparity in the individual's obligation to the two publics is that the individual seeks to gain from the civil public without a moral urge on him to give back to the civil public in return for his benefits. The unwritten law is that it is legitimate and lawful to rob the civil public in order to strengthen the primordial public. This ultimately breads corruption.

Corruption in Nigeria is two-dimensional. This includes outright embezzlement of funds from the civil public, solicitation and acceptance of bribe from individuals seeking services provided by the civil public by those who administer these services. Hence if one steals from the civil public and spends it "wisely" especially to please the primordial public, people think of him as a wise man. But the same primordial public will scream blue murder if one of their members dip into the Union's fund. Such individual will be treated with outrage and even ostracized. Political corruption has been defined as behaviour, which deviates from the formal duties of a public role. C.J. Fredrich also describes political corruption as that behaviour resulting in private gain at the expense of the public. Such behaviour, he goes on to say is "deviant because it violates norms which prevail or which are thought to prevail in a society."

Some definitions have emphasized the misuse of power as a characteristic of corruption. D.II Belay defines corruption as a "general term covering misuse of authority as a result of considerations of personal gains, which need not necessarily be monetary." On the whole, these definitions indicate that corruption not only conflicts with public morality and results to injustice but also subverts the objectives of democracy.

Contractocracy which in its original sense is a system of using the services of experts and specialist to render services to the society at a cost that would be acceptable to both parties is now synonymous with corruption in Nigeria. In the second Republic, for example, contractocracy and corruption manifested themselves in various ways. According to Professor Bayo Adekanye, these include acquisition of enormous wealth by members of the political class, state functionaries and their relations through illegal use or manipulation of public offices; inflation of contract values/costs, contracting projects to companies that were expected to pass on some of their gains to top government functionaries and their representatives in the form of ten percent commission or kickbacks etc. Others include transfers of the political and military class; taking loans from banks or other financial institutions that are rarely repaid or repaid at unrealistic low rates of interest if not deliberately written off; sale of lands to influential members of government at ridiculous prices, sheer extortion; diversion of foreign loans into private bank accounts within and or outside Nigeria; sale of government import licenses to the highest bidder and very often for private gains; personal enrichment from illegal exemptions from tariffs; diversion, sale of/and re-exports of government imported essential commodities for private financial ends; outright embezzlement of public funds; outright theft of moveable materials from government quarters and guest houses etc. The list could go on *ad infinitum*

These and many more have adverse implications for the Nigerian society in which the bureaucratic class is used to drain the wealth of the nation. Our condition can aptly be described as class collaboration on the part of the bourgeoisie and the ruling elite to exploit the resources produced by the working population. These corrupt practices also register the vexed question of ideological fraud on the part of our political elite. It has also affected the psyche of the Nigerian youth. Most youths now yearn for capitalist ethos, as material acquisition has become the yardstick for measuring success. This has concomitantly bred an increase in social ills associated with the "get-rich-quick" syndrome such as armed robbery, drug trafficking advance fee fraud popularly referred to as '419,' prostitution and the like.

Forms Of Corruption In Nigeria

So far I have given a general overview of corruption in Nigeria. Let us at this point be more specific in identifying the various forms of corruption in Nigeria. One of the many areas where we have recorded the highest rate of corruption is the petroleum industry. In 1980 the news was rife that N2.8 billion had been misappropriated from the coffers of the NNPC. The Shehu Shagari government at the period responded by setting up the Crude Oil Sales Tribunal of Inquiry. Justice Ayo Irikefe was at the head of that Tribunal. At the end of the day, Justice Irikefe did not succeed in unearthing the whereabout of the N2.8 billion alleged to have been missing from the account of the Nigerian National Petroleum Corporation (NNPC). Inspite of this failure to nail the ghost that kept this whooping sum of money, the tribunal proved useful in other aspects. For instance the tribunal exposed for the first time, how messy the operations of the NNPC were and how much money was going down the wrong channels. In the Daily Times of Saturday May 24, 1980, Justice Ayo Irikefe was quoted as saying that it is very difficult if not impossible to determine the volume of crude oil being taken away from this country because the oil companies make the NNPC oil inspectors happy... "They give them enough of imported beer to drink and while drinking beer, oil is being pumped and lifted out of the country."

And while the beer-quaffing and oil lifting were going on simultaneously, little was known at the time that there was oil bunkering on a very large scale and that what was coming into the coffers of the government was perhaps just a fraction of what was being drained away. And because Nigeria is a nation where absentmindedness is a virtue, no one seemed to mind that quite a chunk of the nation's wealth was being siphoned away. Perhaps it was the illusion that our oil was in-exhaustible, or nearly so, and that there was more where that oil was coming from, that emboldened the looters and which made those who should have curbed them to look the other way as long as their pockets were brimming with stolen cash. The truth is that the sheep and wolves became penned together and the interests of the sheep and wolves became one and indistinguishable. The looting of the oil wealth has continued unabated with sharp practices to the sector becoming more and more sophisticated each passing day.

So when our producing states jump at recently approved thirteen percent derivation for them, their joy misses the point. It is said or suggested that monthly allocations to these states have increased by over N800 million. I do not know what the states would say or do if they realize that as much as about forty percent of what Nigeria nets from crude oil sales go into wrong hands and pockets. Somewhere in the NNPC, as we are talking here, a racket is going on with the active connivance of our own people. Already some of the state governors in the area are reported as saying that they do not know what to do with the sudden windfall. They are contemplating fatuous projects, which may never be completed. This was exactly what Nigeria did in the '70s and conceived of using her surplus resources in organizing jamborees and playing a generous "Father Christmas".

Tragically, this pervasive practice amounts to subversion of self by self, the arche-type of our predicament. Chinua Achebe correctly observes in his short book, *The Trouble with Nigeria* that corruption in Nigeria has passed "the alarming stage and entered the fatal and critical stage and that Nigeria will die if we keep pretending that she is only slightly indisposed." He further lamented that "the sum of all the fraud committed against the people of Nigeria in the public and private sectors would come to a figure so staggering as to completely boggle the imagination."

Nigeria's report card since independence reads like a parchment of corruption and scroll of mindless iniquities. The grim reality is amplified in the sorry state of our infrastructures, which is grossly dysfunctional and tragically hopeless, basic social services like telephone mortuarise, while our roads are no better than booby traps meant to capture animals of prey. Alongside this hopeless scenario is a double-digit inflation oscillating mercilessly between 100 and 200 percent. Nigeria represents a typical example of the Hobbesian State of nature where life is 'brutish, nasty and short'. Achebe agrees with Thomas Hobbes when he said that, "Nigeria could be a haven for pirates and adventurers... only a character out of Tuttuola's film will pick Nigeria for anything meaningful."

Professor Claude Ake at the 10th Guardian Anniversary lecture painted a grim and grotesque picture of the Nigerian society. According to Ake, Nigeria is a "society of beggars, parasites and bandits". Before he passed on, he saw into time and concluded that Nigeria "cannot know peace or stability, and it cannot be democratic in the real sense. It can only gravitate endlessly as we are doing presently in material poverty and moral regression." Prophetic as Ake sounded, "Nigeria has continued to lumber aimlessly like a behemoth, charting an unknown course at the end of which we may harvest the ruins of a nation destined for greatness but destroyed by a senseless circle of human stupidity, and buffoonery propelled by mindless looting, corruption and unprecedented thievery."

While oil wealth had activated progressive development and economic well being in other oil producing states, ours had become our Archille's Heel. Nigeria's corruption conundrum got to a crescendo during the over three decades of military dictatorship in Nigeria. The military therefore are severally and collectively responsible for the decay and stench of malfeasance that haunt Nigeria today. I have always maintained that military dictatorship is a historical anachronism, an imperiled genre, which share a striking similarity with Fukuyama's illustration of Leninist totalitarianism, in *The End of History* and *The last Man* as a government in which a small cabal of despots rule over the larger public with iron fist and big stick.

Nigeria is the tenth most populous nation in the world. She pumps well over two million barrels of oil a day and that makes her the sixth largest producer of oil in the world and fourth largest in OPEC. Regrettably, Nigeria has vitiated the affirmation of the Nigerian dream through mindless looting and corruption. There is no doubting the fact that the south-south and south-east produce the wealth that sustain this country with over 80 percent of oil coming from the south-south region. Unfortunately the region has never known peace. Outsiders march in unquestioned, exploit these resources and use it to develop their own area. Our people are encouraged to fight themselves with the state providing the weapons of war to the warring communities of the Niger Delta. The environment is inhabitable, putrefied and nauseating and the regions' manifold destiny imperiled by agents of corruption. And yet when we get a crumb of the cake baked in our land and with our sweat and blood, we jump to high heavens forgetting that a labourer is always worthy of his hire and yet in this country, there exists a state where the chief executive is worth billions of naira, and spends all his time outside this country. Civil Service in the state is virtually non-existent. Workers only come to work to prepare vouchers for payment at the end of the month. Every month, the state receives allocation from the Federal government to function. You know as well as I do that this is our oil money being used as charitable funds to run a dry state.

But it is not only in the oil sector that Nigeria is short-changed. The story of the cement scandal is well known but, because of the mind-boggling and utter senselessness of the cement deal, the matter assumes new and fresh verve each time it is mentioned. It is a story that bears repetition. In 1974, the government was eager to prosecute the projects under the Third National Development Plan. In March 1974, the then Nigerian National Supply Company placed order for two million metric tonnes of cement with various firms in the USSR, Romania and the USA to be delivered in 1975. Private cement importers felt out placed by the government initiative and when the cheaper cement from Europe arrived, it was hijacked at sea. The External Affairs Commissioner Okoi Arikpo attributed the piracy to some "unidentified Nigerian businessmen with foreign collaborators." That may be amazing to those who are not familiar with the incident. The Ministry of Defence needed just 2.9 million metric tonnes of cement for its projects but choked the Ports. As is customary, a tribunal of inquiry was set up. The justice M.B. Belgore Tribunal found to its dismay that the method adopted by the Permanent Secretary in the Defence Ministry hardly reflected any known system, since it was not based on any discernible organized procedure. None of the 60 cement contracts considered was awarded by the Ministry's Tenders Board inspite of the fact that most of the contracts were for a sum of fourteen million USD each. The method used merely encouraged a free-for-all bargain by all categories of adventurers known as local agents or local representatives. That was not all. At that time the going price for a tonne of cement was $25 and $15 for freight giving a total of $40, but the price was hiked by government officials to about $115 - an excess of $75 for those involved in the deal.

Regrettably Nigeria has gotten to a stage in which it is no longer possible to differentiate between the armed robbers in our midst and the thieves who pilot the affairs of government. Government appointments are no longer made on the basis of competence and talent, not even on the basis of geo-political and ethno-cultural affiliations but on the basis of the extent to which the appointee can readily adapt to and encourage the depletion of the national wealth. Given such senseless situation, the exceptions of national leaders is no more defined in relation to how they can concretely address the urgent social, political and economic problems in our society but the extent to which they can pillage the common wealth but have thus created institutional structures, which we unashamedly employ in plundering the national resources paving way for the legitimization of corruption, and being a colonial legacy especially at the stage of negotiation for the replacement of colonial masters by the nationalist elite, the mechanisms of corruption have been perfected to a level of statecraft.

Every regime in Nigeria has brought with it its own form of corruption. Under the Gowon regime, Nigeria acquired a reputation as the most benevolent "Father Christmas." It was clear beyond doubt that Nigeria was threading the path of self-destruction. Elsewhere, other oil producing countries did not fold their hands and watch their petro-dollars stolen by agents of corruption. They did not romanticize their potentials; waiting for what anthropologists refer to as "Cargo cult" mentality where one day a ship laden with all the goods they have always dreamed of would come and berth in their habour. They refused to be fooled into believing that oil was an inexhaustible asset and consequently mobilized their resource for meaningful development and spread of wealth among the citizenry. But what did Nigeria do with her oil wealth? Under Gowon, the country spent billions of Naira in relief packages to "needy" African nations. Ordinarily, no one would have raised a finger in protest but for the staggering and glaring evidence of corruption associated with these humanitarian gestures. Various commissions of inquiry including the Justice Mohammed Commission noted that, "the proceeds were cornered by well placed bureaucrats, traditional rulers and business men. An American Economist gave a pungent depiction of battered hopes and frustration when he lamented that for the most vigorous, capable, resourceful, well-connected and lucky entrepreneurs (including politicians, civil servants and army officers), a productive economic activity, namely the creation of wealth and real income has faded in appeal. Access to and manipulation of the government spending process has become the golden gateway to fortune. There was no doubting the fact that the Gowon regime had reached the dreaded Peters principle - a point where the government was bereft of ideas. The nation groaned under the weight of institutionalized corruption and socio-economic rot.

General Ramat Muhammad sacked the Gowon regime and embarked upon a cleansing exercise. The leadership quality was different even though the rulership was short. Sanity for the first time was brought to bear on the system. Corrupt, inept and unproductive military officers were fired, retired or reprimanded. Thousands of civil servants lost their jobs for reasons of corruption among others. There was discipline in the system. It radiated from the hierarchy of the Governor to the mass base of the governed. Nigerians appreciated the change. The country had a sense of direction, purposeful leadership and a dynamic militant foreign policy. His short-lived regime paved the way for the continuation of plundering and mismanagement of our enormous resources.

Consequently, we moved from the celebrated cement scandal to the N300 million fertilizer scandal and yet again to rice scandal. "Operation Feed the Nation" was conceived of good intention but its planning and execution was riddled with fraud, mismanagement, extortion and corruption. The government bureaucrats, contractors and middlemen inflated the project costs in order to enrich themselves. Obsolete farm machinery were imported for the prices of new ones and the wrong type of fertilizer purely for the gain motif rather than appropriateness. Amidst this high importation of agricultural imputs, our import content of food was also rising. Nigerian economy was virtually thrown open for dubious foreign investors. Nigeria's attempt at industrialization was left at the mercy of contractors and international wheeler-dealers who found ready allies among the members of the country's ruling class.

When we changed the leadership, it was to welcome the Second Republic with its executive presidential system. It was a civilian government that openly legitimized election rigging, corruption in high places, adoration of ineptitude and incompetence, plundering of the treasury, fraud and cover up and total mismanagement of the economy. This inexorably led to the collapse of our public utility. We changed from the failed Operation Feed the Nation to the warped Green Revolution. Billions of oil money were wasted on the project only to produce hunger and mass poverty. The Second Republic under Shagari spent a whopping N2 billion for the development of the Federal Capital Territory, Abuja only to develop a new list of party financiers through illegal and fraudulent contract awards. Most of the contracts were never executed while the contractors disappeared into thin air with millions of naira of moblization fees to build new houses, buy new cars, marry new wives and take numerous chieftaincy titles. It was a regime that placed little or no emphasis on the preservation of our valuable culture and records. To cover up corruption and profligacy, many of our natural monuments went up in flames. The fire at the Ministry of External Affairs and the Nigerian External Telecommunications were ample examples of this sad reality.

From December 31, 1983 when Generals Muhammadu Buhari and Tunde Idiagbon sacked the civilian government of Shehu Shagari, the nation experienced one form of military dictatorship after another. It was during this period, which terminated on 29 May 1999 that corruption and "settlement" became accepted politics of government. So much has been said and written about Babangida and Abacha years that I cannot go over that period here. Ladies and gentlemen, you will agree with me that ours is no more corruption but blatant stealing. We have had cases where a Minister complains to the Head of State that he was broke and the Head of State would "dash" him as much as 30 million Deutschmark. We have had instances where a Head of State openly legitimizes corruption and treasury looting, setting the pace by diverting billions of our oil money to build for himself a 50-bedroom mansion. We have had cases where Abacha gives his son as much as 700M USD in cash to keep for him or as gift. For your information, 700M USD will pay the salaries of One million Nigerian workers on GL.1 at N5500 for 11 years. And yet somebody had the guts to steal that much from our common wealth when retired workers are not paid their pensions and gratuities; sacked ones are not paid in lieu of notice and Nigerian workers are dying in their thousands. This is indeed lamentable and can only be described as economic genocide against millions of Nigerians. I have articulated these years of corruption and mindless looting and state terrorism in my book *Nigeria: The Stolen Billions* copies of which are available here today.

Let me end this section of the paper by reiterating that corruption and mismanagement have eaten deep into the core of the Nigerian state and have become a tragic but regular part of the national sensibility and consciousness. Of course, the future is bleak for the country and its people if this is the legacy that will be handed over to the future generation. The graveness of the situation does not call for clowning or messianic pretensions but for concerted efforts on our part to re-orientate our minds, have new attitudes and new values. This must start from the government circles. When the government is not only transparent but seen to be transparent, the radiation will naturally affect every facet of our national life down the ladder.

But even as we hope for a better Nigeria - a Nigeria where God-fearing leaders would pilot the affairs of state; where no crook or armed bandit will be in government, we must not fail to ask the fundamental question - Why has Nigeria been overwhelmed by this level of corruption? In my quiet times I have seriously ruminated on this question and have identified two postulations to its explanation.

The first is the tremendous amount of wealth, which a generous providence poured into our coffers immediately after the civil war. This wealth, which came from oil was channeled to the centre. Instead of sharing this wealth according to the principles of federalism, which our founding fathers laid down, the federal military government began to share the wealth like spoils of war and took everything wholesale. This was a government that was desperately in search of fund; going around with cap in hand for fund to prosecute the civil war. Suddenly after the war there was oil boom. The boom was stupendous and overwhelmed the Gowon regime to the extent that Gowon told the world that Nigeria had so much money that it did not know how to spend but know how to steal.

The situation could not have been different given the fact that the only ethnic group that rose in challenge to this monumental thievery and squandering of our common wealth had been silenced - So it seemed. *Ndigbo* were cast in the rile of felon; a wrecker of the country. With such stigma, Nigeria conspired to deal *Ndigbo* a lethal blow. When the monumental looting started, the military felt that no person could stop it. The only obstacle to the total routing of the Niger-Delta has been rendered impotent. That was why the Abacha junta could walk into Ogoniland, pluck Ken Saro-Wiwa and many others and slaughtered them. That is why the weapons of war are constantly directed at this region to subdue and cow us into submission while the mindless looting and plundering of our oil wealth continues unabated. In defeating the Igbo, the military defeated the whole Nigeria so they assumed; just to loot.

Another point of explanation is the over centralization of power at the centre. The emergence of the military in governance dragged the country into the orbit of unitarism and rendered our federalist structures superficial and dysfunctional. The military who usurped power were not trained for political leadership. Rather, they were trained in military command and obey system with a lot of rigidity and centralized command. This military philosophy was brought to bear on the polity. General Aguiyi Ironsi was the first person who tried to enthrone the unitary system of government. In the counter-coup of 1966, one of the reasons given for the murder of Aguiyi Ironsi by Gowon and his colleagues was the practice of Unitarism. Surprisingly after seizing power, Gowon and his cohorts became even more unitary than Ironsi intended. Consequently, the new military regime and subsequent ones found itself in an unusual war - the war of managing a politically and culturally diverse society like ours. To survive this war, the junta had tremendous powers to appropriate our oil wealth without question. The consequence is that the military has bequeathed to the civilians this authoritarian tendency and Nigeria has continued to be managed in unitary terms.

Again the question comes - what do we do? The answer again is simple. We must, as a matter of urgency go back to the practice of true federalism. How do we get back to the true principles of federalism? This brings us to the contentious question of re-structuring which case I have argued below.

The Case for Restructuring

The question about restructuring this country has been recorded, and correctly so, as the only way Nigeria can move forward. We can no longer shy away from this obvious reality.

From every corner of our society the persistent feeling of anger, frustration, marginalization and increasing alienation rear their ugly heads. Very many concerned Nigerians have called for a radical loosening of the powers of the centre or negotiated dismemberment of the country. The artificiality that is Nigeria has been acknowledged by all and sundry as a big mistake. However, I am sure that as many as are calling for a negotiated Nigeria only when it is restructured in such a manner as to reflect the principles of true federalism, where every ethnic nationality will have unhindered access and control over its resources. I alongside other patriotic Nigerians are convinced that for this country to remain relevant and avoid a catastrophe, there must be a Sovereign National Conference where issues appertaining to the Nigerian being will be discussed without let or hindrance.

Presently the South-West, South-South and South-East have agreed on the need for the following:-

- Proper restructuring of the country along the lines of true federalism. This is the only hope left for the country to salvage whatever is left of her. The high voltage ethnic conflicts and religious intolerance can only be resolved through a Sovereign National Conference.

- Proper principles of derivation formula where every ethnic nationality will control whatever it owns as resources.
- Self-determination of each ethnic nationality based on the foregoing derivation principle. In 1966, delegates from all the regions at the constitutional conference in Lagos agreed on this, which the North proposed and was adopted by all the other regions.
- Convocation of a SNC where all these issues will be discussed *sans* emotion.
- Total rejection of the 1999 Constitution on the ground that it is a military Constitution, which does not reflect the wishes of the people.

Recall that at independence, our founding fathers adopted federalism as an imperative constitutional framework for the continued existence of the country. These forerunners, we must admit, did their best to have and to hold the country under a federalist structure and there was a good degree of healthy competition among the regions.

The emergence of the military triggered a sustained departure from the true principles of Federalism. Like magicians, the various military junta in Nigeria embarked upon the production and imposition of militarized constitutions based on the military ethics of command and obey system. The so-called states created by the military are nothing but fiefdoms for the creation of mandarin millionaires. The 1999 Constitution is a striking example of a narzist document fashioned for the emergence of a civilian despot with its in - built contradictions to democratic governance. In fact the 1999 Constitution was meant for the perpetuation of Sani Abacha in office, it was never intended for any civilized society. It is indeed regrettable that the present Federal Government inherited that contraption. In all its facets, that Constitution is a maniacal contraption, a distorted and paranoid document, a rag-tag document that only Abacha's decree manufacturing company 'PLC' could have rolled out. It eliminated Nigerians and tended to *zombify* them.

With such alienation, it is not surprising that the various ethnic nationalities and other segments of our society have become increasingly restive and are crying for a change. They want to be able to manage their own affairs at the level of greatest impact of government on their lives. Virtually, every ethnic group in Nigeria has a *prima facie* case on the need for a SNC. From the Niger-Delta to the Igbos through the Yorubas and even the North, there is a persistent quest for the restructuring of the country based on a SNC.

In the Niger-Delta for example, the land has been pillaged, their resources stolen, their people killed and maimed with careless abandon. The living conditions of the people of the Niger-Delta have become increasingly intolerable and the people have concomitantly become edgy and frustrated.

Over time especially since after the civil war, marginalisation and near exclusion have become a way of life for *Ndigbo*. *Ndigbo* have been effectively sidelined in every sphere of our national life. The Nigerian Army for instance is an ethnic army. Presently, no Igbo is considered worthy of appointment as a Service Chief inspite of the fact that *Ndigbo* constitute the largest ethnic group in Nigeria. In the Police, Customs and Excise, Airways and other Federal parastatals, the story is the same for *Ndigbo*. In the whole of Igboland, there is no NEPA station as we have in Kainji, Afam and Egbin in Lagos. The Oji-River Thermal Power station has since turned into the official residence of lizards, rats and snakes.

There is the question of the attempt by the Abacha junta to annihilate the entire Yoruba race by ethnicizing the annulment of the June 12, 1993 presidential election. In trying to do this, Nigerians were visited with unpardonable economic and physical genocide.

There is equally the current process of islamization of the core north. There is of course nothing wrong with that exercise rather it has helped to define the citizenship question and exposed the pontifications about one Nigeria as a ruse, hollow aberration and unmitigated hypocrisy.

I have always asked the question -why is Nigeria in such quagmire? And my conclusion has always been that our systemic contradictions are not strange ailments inflicted upon us by some supernatural force, but have their roots in the warped contraption that is Nigeria. I have always maintained based on historical and empirical realities, that the determining currents of history are language, culture, religion and class cleavages to a lesser extent. It is indeed regrettable that our leaders have persistently pandered to the regressive dictates of these determinants of history and social forces. By so doing they have refused to address the root cause of our problems.

I am convinced that it is only through a SNC that Nigerians can and between themselves author a constitution, which will usher in an authentic Federal Nigeria. The 1999 Constitution was never intended to be amended because of the frustrating stumbling blocks and convolutions of the amendments.

A conference of the ethnic nationalities will afford us the opportunity to cross-fertilize ideas. It is sovereign because what is agreed upon is binding. Every nationality will infuse its will into the resolutions of the conference with a substance, which need not be violated by the will of others. SNC is not secession nor will it create leadership vacuum. A progressive Nigeria can only be inaugurated through an unfitted SNC devoid of any form of encumbrance. SNC means a decisive end to ethnic conflicts in Nigeria, the end of mutual suspicion and perpetual subversion. It will be the end of a neo-colonial Nigeria and the birth of a new Nigeria.

It is, therefore in relation to the foregoing variables that we can understand and historically evaluate the process called SNC. To neglect the crucial nature of this perspective is to avoid coming to terms with the essence of Nigerian historical experience and the socio-political condition which provoked upheavals and tensions because, SNC as a process of change denoted a radical departure from the past that has failed to make the present meaningful. It will succeed in creating a new social order, a new configuration that will be superior in content and form than the present one. SNC connotes positive change for Nigeria because it is a process born out of historical contradictions. Its process is immutable and the final outcome will be inviolable.

Finally, I am confident in stating that Nigeria has no alternative to SNC. It is a great historical moment, which will soon occur for the simple reason that ethnic conflicts, religious conflicts and other systemic defects in our political system have stymied us in an avoidable quagmire.

I do not have any doubt in my mind that Mr. President appreciates the fact that for this country to land on safe ground, there is no alternative to SNC. As a matter of fact, it is SNC that will provide a safe landing platform for Nigeria. It is an enormous responsibility with history and circumstances. There lies the safety of Nigeria and our corporate existence.

Again I thank you for this opportunity to make my patriotic contributions to the survival and growth of our nation. I hope I have succeeded in acquitting myself with your fruitful deliberations.

Thank You.

Chapter Three

The Nigerian State As An Instrument of Corruption

Akani Christian[*]

Introduction

Every epoch has its own conflicts. The resolution of these conflicts, mostly socially-determined expose the backwardness or development of that epoch.

The seventeenth century, particularly in Britain marked the rosy dawn of capitalist development. The bourgeois revolution of 1688 in Britain re-enacted the prominence of natural law and liberty. These concepts exposed by the seventeenth century theorists especially John Locke, indirectly justified and approved the extension and expansion of capitalist ethos in other countries.

All this was encapsulated in the enlightenment movement where "Freedom, Equality and Fraternity" became the sweeping slogan of the French Revolution of 1789. Other countries have emulated the technique of industrial expansion with the influence and rise of the middle class.

By the nineteenth and twentieth centuries, capitalism had completely appropriated the natural resources of the unoccupied world. This was through gunboat diplomacy, war, and crude force. It eventually marked the emergence of colonialism and imperialism. Colonialism simply means the total subjugation of one country by another. According to Walter Rodney "Colonialism was not merely a system of exploitation, but one whose essential purpose was to repatriate the profits to the so-called mother country."[1]

For more than sixty years, Africa laboured under the strong might of colonialism as it struggled, fought and won independence. Fortunately, by the turn of the twentieth

---

[*] Akani Christian is the Executive Director of Institute of Academic Freedom in Nigeria.

[1] Walter Rodney, *How Europe undeveloped Africa* (London: Bogle- L'Ouverture Publications, 1972) P. 162.

century, South Africa became free. This was a death knell to the last vestiges of colonialism in Africa.

Interestingly, by the late twentieth and early twenty-first centuries, a new epoch had emerged. This is the epoch of human rights and democracy.

These concepts, although not novel in the conscience of the world have come to assume a totally different dimension. They have become a standard to measure the practice and actions of nation states. The international community has come to see them as part and parcel of its norm which every rational state must adopt. This was why General Sani Abacha's terroristic dictatorship was roundly condemned. It is important to state that these two concepts cannot triumph with the bold efflorescence of endemic corruption. They are not only antithetical, but have goals which are completely irreconcilable.

Corruption simply means the debasement or pervasion of an approved process, for the purpose of gaining an advantage which in most cases is selfish and personal. It is a dishonest and putrid way of getting things, which ordinarily could not have been got. It has the capacity of permeating man's psyche and if not nipped in the bud, it becomes part of his norms, mores and hallowed conventions as it is in Nigeria.

This explains why a corrupt-ridden state or community can hardly observe democracy and human rights. Those who benefit by it can hardly be expected to make any genuine effort to stop it. Examples abound in the country.

This paper will critically examine to what extent the Nigerian State has aided the consolidation of corruption in our body politic.

What is the State

The concept of the state is not strange in social discourse. This is not surprising because it is the pivot of social, political and legal activities in every formation.

To objectively comprehend the various events which unfold in the society, we need to take a critical examination of the

THE NIGERIAN STATE AS AN INSTRUMENT OF CORRUPTION 31

State. Unfortunately, an acceptable definition of this concept has not arisen. But its historical mission is not in doubt.

Many political theorists conceptualise the state as a natural necessity. This is because man is a productive being. This natural urge to reproduce himself may conflict with his neighbours. The state therefore, is necessary to regulate and mediate this crisis. Aristotle sees the state as the epic of his teleological movement. To him, the formation of the state which started from the family is the completion of the natural movement and superintends over the affairs of people impartially.

It is against this background that we can appreciate the State in the eyes of the Greeks. According to Pericle, any person who does not participate in the affairs of the State is not only a useless character but an idiot. To them, the State is the centre of all social, religious, political and economic activities, which binds people together. It is an institution established in the interest of the society as a whole for the purpose of mediating and reconciling the antagonisms to which social existence inevitably gives rise.[2]

Fredrick Hegel reaffirmed the supremacy and natural emergence of the state in his works. According to him, the state is absolutely rational - "...the state is the actuality of the ethical idea". It is within the prism of the State that man can maximize his potentials. This is why he sees the state as "mind objectified, genuine individuality and an ethical life." For Hegel, the State is not a product of man's history, but "is the idea of spirit in the external manifestation of human will and its freedom."[3]

It is, therefore not stupendous that this impartial and naturally-ordained conception of the State has permeated the thought of liberal writers. According to them, "the State is responsible for the maintenance of law and order by merely balancing things out between elite groups."

---

[2] Paul M. Sweezy, *The Theory of capitalist Development* (London: Monthly Review Press, 1970) P. 240.
[3] Samuel E. Stump, *Philosophy: History and Problems* (New York: MC- Graw - Hill Book Company, 1971). P.337.

It maintains order and settles quarrels and conflicts in society. It assumes that the underlying class structure of a society, or what comes to the same thing, the system of property relation is an immutable datum like the order of nature itself.[4]

By the turn of the nineteenth century, this bourgeois conception of the State became unfashionable because of its marked limitations. It completely blanketed the character of property accumulation. The class configuration of the society and the social relations which filliped reactions and conflicts remained unmentioned. Society was seen as a homogenous and free people, subjecting themselves to an impartial state.

These limitations and the contradictions of capitalism, led to the Marxian conception of the state. It was diametrically opposed to the liberal thought.

In the social production of material resources, men enter into production relations. These relations determine the nature of surplus produced, and its appropriation and consumption. It also controlled corresponding superstructural norms such as law, religion and ideas. The class that is predominant in the control of the produced surplus permeates the entire society through state apparatuses such as the Police, Prison, Judiciary, Army and Customs. Without the State, they cannot maintain and consolidate their relationship, which is often exploitative.

> The state itself is created by actual material relationship concerning property rights, the division of labour, class structure and the relation of property.[5]

According to V.I. Lenin, the state has not always existed,

> It appears wherever and whenever there is a division of society into classes, ...and whenever exploiters and exploited appear.[6]

In other words, the existence of the State shows vividly the division of the society into two or more hostile and antagonistic

---

[4] Paul M Sweedy *op cit* P.24.

[5] Akani Christian, the State Private Property and the dominant class in Economy Uniport; M.Sc. Thesis, Sept. 1992 P.24.

[6] V.I. Lenin, *Marx, Angles Marxism*, (Peking: Foreign Language Press 1978) p. 508.

groups. The group that controls the state apparatuses uses it to advance and consolidate its own interest. The state, therefore is not impartial and natural. The doctrine of the State serves as a justification of the existence of exploitation, a justification of the existence of capitalism.[7]

The above is anchored on the fact that,

> History shows that the State as a special apparatus for coercing people arose only wherever and whenever there appeared a division of society into classes, that is a division into groups of people some of which were permanently in a position to appropriate the labour of others, where some people exploited others.[8]

Marxist conception of the State is emphatically an instrument for the continuous expansion of bourgeois economic interest and frontiers. This is why it does not see anything that would protect the interest of the exploited within its prism. It is just 'the executive committee for managing the affairs of the bourgeoisie', 'a machine for the oppression of one class by another, a machine for holding in obedience to one class other subordinated class'.[9]

All populist actions and democratic endeavours of the State do not alter its essence because the ownership of means of production still remains in the hands of a few.

Universal suffrage, a Constituent Assembly, Parliament are merely promissory note, which does not alter the essence of the matter.[10] This anti-people and extreme bourgesification of the State has been rejected by later theorists. It may be difficult to say that the State at all times work essentially for the interest of the dominant class. According to Eme Ekekwe;

> To leave the matter thus, would however, be to harbour a simplistic and vulgarised conception of the State. It would be quite difficult, if indeed possible at all for the state to be a mere instrument of the ruling class

---

[7] Ibid p25.
[8] Ibid P.26.
[9] Ibid P.27.
[10] Ibid.

since infact that class is one in which is internally divided and subject to serious intra-class competition.[11]

It is important to state that the class that controls the state apparatus is not a homogenous and crisis-free one. Some of them may not own any means of production.

In other to sustain their control of the society, they occasionally make some concessions and compromises. On the face of it, this is a defeat of the hegemonic class. The long run effect of this is that it helps in the permeation of the civil society and consolidation of the State ideas. The Ten Hours Bill in 1864 was acclaimed by Marx as a victory of political economy of labour. The repeal of the Corn Law of 1815 in 1846 and some of the populist measures of Ibrahim Babangida and the defensive radicalism of some African leaders, attest clearly to the fact that the State does not always work according to the command and behest of the bourgeois class.

Nevertheless, every State has a class character. The class that is in control of a State must of necessity use it to advance and project its interest and appropriate resources. In the case of a bourgeois State, it is the capitalists, while in a socialist state the people through the dictatorship of the proletariat.

The state, therefore, is not impartial, it functions for the interest of the ruling class. Its historical antecedents transparently demonstrate this fact. This is why Claude Ake noted that:

> The State, is a specific modality of class domination, in which class is mediated by commodity exchange so that the system of institutional mechanism of domination is differentiated from the ruling class and even the society appear as an objective force standing alongside society.[12]

Through periodic elections and commodity exchange, State becomes relatively autonomous of the civil society and wears the cloak of impartiality. But it is by no means independent of the mode of production. This is because it is within this category

[11] Ibid P27.
[12] Ibid P27.

that the exploitative tendency and combative character of the state becomes obviously manifest. It is against this background that Antonio Gramsi noted that;

> a state is the entire complex of political and theoretical activities within which the ruling class not only justifies and maintains its dominance, but manages to win the entire consent of those over whom it rules.[13]

The Nigerian state is a colonial creation. Colonialism manipulated and subjected the hitherto autonomous communities in a bid to achieve its primary objective. This was the maximum appropriation of raw materials. Negative antics and hard-hitting procedures were consciously employed to weaken the strength of the people. The controllers of the colonial State were hard-headed in their determination to see communities bow before the strength of their colonial forces.

The result was that capitalist etiqette permeated the people, especially through the colonial education. Its receivers saw themselves more in the guise of the colonisers than their cultural root, as in the French policy of assimilation.

It was, therefore, not stupendous that by the time independence was granted on 1st October 1960, a coterie of people had emerged as the mouthpiece of the people. They were culturally cut off from their people. Some of them saw the western world-view and capitalist ethics as a fact of life.

Above all, the disjointed and disarticulated structure of the economy was not overhauled. This made nonsense of the hallowed independence. The State still depended on one of the heaviest manifestations of oppressive ideology, influenced by the vicissitudes and contradictions of global capitalist economy, porous productive base and largely consuming what it does not produce. The aftermath of this was peripheralization in the international division of labour and complete loss of relative autonomy.

There was no difference between state interest and the interest of its controllers. This made the state become part and

---

[13] Ibid.

parcel of the internal struggles and divisions in the civil society. An instrument to realise their dreams.

According to Samuel Egwu, the Nigerian State primarily, promotes and defends the interest of imperialism.[14] It is this attempt to promote the interest of imperialist forces, that makes the Nigerian State objectionable in the mind of the people. This explains the elbow room granted to them for their activities. From our discussion thus far, we can deduce that:

(1)   The Nigerian State emerged after long years of Colonial rule.

(2)   It is controlled by coterie of men who are endemically individualistic, with a tenuous productive base, but lavishly ostentatious.

(3)   With a rentier disposition that enjoys the collection of rents and royalties from T.N.Cs. This rent mentality has permeated the consciousness of many Nigerians that rent agents have become brisk business in the economy.

(5)   Completely lacks any iota of relative autonomy as it is directly involved in daily conflicts in the civil society.

With the above attributes of the Nigerian State, let us examine how these have aided in the efflorescence of corruption in the country.

The State and Corruption

Corruption is the deliberate and conscious pervasion of an official process to fulfil a personal advantage. It is obtaining material enrichment or opportunities --- for oneself and/or for others through the use of public office or personal connection in ways other than those publicly acknowledged through the rules and procedures of office.[15]

Every mode of production introduces its own superstructural ethics. Capitalism which is anchored on the

---

[14] Samuel Egwu, 'The Origin, Nature and Politics of the Niger Delta Crisis The consequence of violence of the future of youths, Workshop on Re-orientation in the Niger Delta organised by the Centre for the Prevention and Control of Violence. May 1 - 3, 2000 Uyo, Akwa Ibom State, P.2.

[15] Eme Ekekwe, *Class and state in Nigeria* (Lagos: Longman 1986) P. 113.

private ownership of means of production aims at an end. This end is the maximization of profit. In achieving this goal, therefore, the capitalist engaged in all kinds of things including killing, war and corruption. The history of colonialism and the imperialist activities of transnational corporations are pellucid examples.

Corruption accelerates the engine of capitalist mode of production because of the economic and political benefits. In other words, the more capitalism expands, the more corruption expands, and the more it becomes sophisticated depending on the level of socio-economic development.

According to Ekekwe:

> Corruption necessarily exists in and is encouraged, by every capitalist economy, since in such an economic system the drive and competition for private profit and capital accumulation are the motor.[16]

Since the propensity to engage in private accumulation of wealth is extremely high, and the philosophy of the bourgeois class is rooted in the Spencerian principle of 'survival of the fittest', no stone is left unturned, no land is left unoccupied and no obstacle is left unremoved in the drive for profit maximization. The bourgeois class becomes so fixated with money that they worship it with a 'greater single mindedness'. Ethical values, morality, bond of relationship and religious passions become after thoughts in the race for capitalist accumulation. These were demonstrated by the English bourgeois class. According to Fredick Engles:

> I have never seen a class so deeply demoralised, so incurably debased by selfishness, so corroded within and so incapable of progress as the English bourgeoisie.[17]

It was against this background that Ekekwe emphatically stated that:

> I consider corruption as very much part of what may be called here the 'economic culture' of the capitalist system. This is to say, corruption is

---

[16] Ibid.
[17] Fredrick Engels, *The Condition of the Working Class in England* (Moscow: Progress Publishers, 1980) P.275.

part of the values, attitudes, skills and orientation that are at play for the maintenance of the system.[18]

Our analysis will examine different regimes.

Sir Tafawa Balewa 1960-1966

This period was the most tumultuous in the political history of the country. It also ushered the dawn of independence, which heralded infinite joy and hope. But these became mere wishful thinking as the neo-colonial foundation and structure of the state strongly limited its power of independence.
According to Osoba:

> Neo-colonialism is not just a communist or a radical nationalist slogan. It was the strategy devised by the departing colonial powers to recoup their loss of direct political control in the emergent nations by consolidating and even enhancing their traditional economic influence and control.[19]

This made Balewa's government to be weak, pro-western and completely lost on how to move the country out of its colonial dependence. The result was that the opposition was tortured, arrested and detained with the instruments of the state. The 1964 and 65 elections were cases in point.

The ruling party effectively used the apparatus of the State to corruptly entrench itself in office. Opposing candidates were outrightly denied necessary electoral papers. Many candidates were fraudulently returned unopposed even when serious opposing candidates had emerged.

Ikejiani stated that if the 1964 elections were ridiculous, the 1965 machiavellian electioneering was sinister and totally unacceptable in its claim[20]. Violence erupted as the 'election was marked by all forms of fraud'. The chairman of the Electoral Commission, Chief Esua, publicly remarked "that it was beyond this Commission to guarantee free and fair election."

---

[18] Eme Ekekwe, Op Cit P. 114.
[19] Toyin Falola, Julius Ihonvbere (Ed) *Nigeria and the International Capitalists System.* (London: Lynne Rienner Publishers 1988) P.18.
[20] O. Ikejiani, M. O. Ikejiani, *Nigeria Political Imperative* (Enugu, Fourth Dimension Publishers 1986) P. 109.

In 1962, the intra-party crisis in the Action Group Party so engaged the whole Western Region that a state of emergency was declared by the Federal Government. A commission of inquiry headed by Justice G.B. Coker noted that:

> We also came across evidence regarding some dishonest and callous politicians who mortgaged their consciences to dishonesty.[21]

Chief Obafemi Awolowo was subsequently charged for treason and imprisoned for ten years. Delivering his judgement, Justice Sowemimo declared that;

> On the evidence before me it would appear that politics generally in Nigeria has been conducted with a certain amount of bitterness and vindictiveness. On the evidence it appears that a person who belongs to a party becomes an enemy of another who belongs to another party.[22]

> '...the shortest cut to affluence and influence is through politics. Politics means money and money means politics...'

The raging violence in all parts of the country as a result of the state-sponsored pervasion of electoral processes and administration created an enabling environment for the militarisation of the country's political life.

According to Major Chukwuma Nzeogwu on January 15, 1966;

> ...our enemies are political profiteers, swindlers, the men in high and low places that seek to keep the country divided permanently so that they can remain in the office as Ministers and VIP's of waste, the tribalists, the nepotistic, those that make the country big for nothing before international circles, those that have corrupted our society and put the Nigerian political calendar back by words and deeds.[23]

Major General Aguiyi Ironsi never made any appreciable impact before General Gowon took over in July 1966. The General Gowon era (1966 – 1975) had unique characteristics.

---

[21] James O. Ojiako, *Nigeria Yesterday, Today and* ... (Onitsha: African Educational Publishers Nigeria Ltd 1981) P. 125.

[22] Akani Christian, *My Ordeal. A Prison Memoir of a Student Artist*. (Port-Harcourt: Jeson Books 1994) P. 29.

[23] Arthur Nwankwo, *Nigeria, The Stolen Billions* (Enugu: Fourth Dimension Published 1999) P.25.

Apart from being a period the country witnessed an unprecedented oil boom and the unregulated inflow of petro-dollars, it fought a fratricidal war which almost reduced the country to shreds. About one million people were killed. It is also on record that it was the regime that laid a firm foundation for graft, corruption and shameless embezzlement of state funds.

From N1.8m realised from oil in 1958, it multiplied to N509.6m in 1970. This windfall was marvelous to the controllers of state power. Gowon once stated that Nigeria's problem was not money, but how to spend it. It set the stage for the embezzlement of money through fraudulent activities. [24] He could not chastise his lieutenants found guilty of brazen corruption. He 'suffered from power fatigue, and ran out of ideas...' and became innately weak. Corruption became a national institution, a festering wound that would continue to embarrass and scandalise Nigerians.

According to General Murtala Mohammed, all ex-military governors and the former administration of East Central State with the exception of two were found to have grossly abused their offices and guilty of several irregular practices. Those of them who wore uniforms betrayed the ethics of their profession and they are a disgrace to their professions. They should be ashamed of themselves.[25] Most of them lost properties ranging from land, money and houses to the State.

Rationalizing the motive for the removal of Gowon, General Murtala Mohammed stated that the nation had been groping in the dark and the situation would inevitably result in chaos and bloodshed. Lack of consultation, indecision, indiscipline and even neglect characterised the state of affairs. To give the nation a new lease of life, it was decided to remove General Gowon.[26]

Unfortunately, on 13th February 1976, General Mohammed was killed in a failed coup d' tat by Lt. Col. Dimka. This led to the emergence of General Olusegun Obasanjo 1976-

---

[24] Ibid P.30.
[25] *Africa Concord* April, 1 1990, Vol.5 No. 48 P. 27.
[26] Ikejiani Op. Cit P. 165 –166.

79. The regime was temporarily sustained by its populist commitment. But it gradually lost steam. The regime engaged in many white elephant projects such as the Operation Feed the Nation (OFN), hosting of World Scout Jamboree, Festival of Arts and Culture-Festac 77. The result was colossal deficit especially in the oil industry. This was how the sum of N2.8b belonging to the Nigerian National Petroleum Company was found to be missing. According to Ayo Irekefe panel:

> There is no independent system in existence at the present time for collaborating the figures of crude oil produced neither at the NNPC nor the Federal Ministry of Finance.[27]

Falola and Julius, noted that:

> Corruption and waste, particularly over inflated contracts, increased food and capital goods imports all contributed to constantly depleting the country's foreign exchange earnings thus necessitating internal and external borrowing.[28]

Between 1975 - 76 fiscal year, there was a deficit of N0.8m in the first nine months of the fiscal year. [29] The Obasanjo era totally deviated from the defensive radicalism of the Murtala period, and dissociated itself from internal over heating of the corrupt order.

The fight against corruption which was hitherto pursued with much vigour under Murtala fizzled out into empty rhetoric and harmless rituals.[30] Army Generals and those connected to the military made extraordinary money from contracts and other favoured gifts.

By the time Obasanjo handed over to Alhaji Shehu Shagari, on 1st October 1979,

---

[27] Toyin Falola, Julius Ihonvbere, *The Rise and Fall of Nigeria Second Republic 1979 –84* London Zed Books Ltd, 1985) P.93.

[28] G.O. Nwankwo, *Nigeria and OPEC To Be or Not To Be* (Ibadan: African Universities Press 1983) P.&.

[29] Ibid.

[30] Arthur Nwankwo Op. Cit P. 35.

The Nigerian economy was already on the brink of collapse. Inflation was well over 30%, unemployment and labour unrest were on the increase and the import bill was over N600m per month.[31]

Elected Assemblymen saw their position as an opportunity to consolidate their economic foundation. They completely abandoned their statutory responsibility and went after money wherever it could be found. It was a childish dance of vanity, as things were done off the cuff. The President demonstrated a besotted disposition, and seemed to lack control of events.

> According to Dele Giwa, 'those who followed the gutter activities of the National Assembly knew that it would be possible to find something defying to say about that body beyond the inclination to describe it as the theatre of absurd.[32]

By 1982, they had spent more than N3m on telephone calls. In the same vein, the one week inter-parliamentary conference which took place in Lagos gulped more than N3m.

The Alhaji Yinusa Paiko panel which investigated the Home Committee on Finance in respect of S.G.S, a Swiss company, discovered that;

> The Committee members were not only extravagantly entertained by SGS but that it also offered them luxuries far beyond the norms of ordinary business hospitality[33].

One convenient way through which the Executive penetrated the Assembly was through the President's Liaison Officers. These officers were '...particularly notorious for... unbridled and indiscreet manner of distributing money amongst legislators'. Money was the ultimate goal, and any action that does not attract financial benefit was relegated to the background.

This was why overseas trips to 'learn' the Presidential System were important. In two years about N2m had on overseas trips.

---

[31] Toyin Falota Julius, Ihonvbere, (Ed) *Op. cit* 105.
[32] Dickon Ageda (Ed) *Corruption and the Stability of The Third Republic* (Lagos: Perception Communications 1993) P.20.
[33] Ibid P.21.

According to Nwankwo;

> Between the early 1970's and 1980's, about $100b of oil flowed into
> Nigeria's treasury, a large chunk ended up in private bank accounts in
> Europe and North America.[34]

Internal debt of N300m was over inflated to N7.86b. The
difference went to individual accounts in Europe. Corruption
had deepened into the marrows that not even the hypocritical
Shagari's Ethical Revolution could flush it out. By the end of
1980, the financial mismanagement and reckless importation of
goods have begun to have an impact on the Nigerian Society. In
1979, imports increased from N722b to N1.2m in 1981.[35]
Falola and Julius noted that:

> Corruption was not, however limited to contract inflation. The Second
> Republic was notorious for fraud: payment of huge sums of money to
> ghost workers; importation of fake products. (mud and sand) in order to
> obtain foreign exchange; outright stealing of government property;
> illegal transfer of money to private accounts.[36]

Not surprisingly, all these corrupt and indisciplined
practices led to the introduction of austerity measures through
the Economic Stabilization Act of 1982. By 1983, Shagari sadly
stated that,

> I intend to revamp the economy and continue to pilot our nation on the
> path to political stability as well as provide increased development in
> order to improve the quality of life and security of the individual.[37]

The Shagari Government's score card was a parchment of
corruption and iniquities and a sad commentary on how
unpatriotic leaders would sink a nation to an irredeemable abyss
of perdition.[38]

Shagari's government was internally confused and patently
corrupt. There was no aspect of the society that was healthy.

---

[34] Arthur Nwankwo *Op Cit* P.46.
[35] Falola and Julius Ihonvbere *Op Cit* at P.105.
[36] Ibid P. 108.
[37] Ibid P. 117.
[38] Arthur Nwankwo *Op. Cit* P48 –49.

These necessitated his overthrow on December 1983 by General Mohammadu Buhari.

General Mohammadu Buhari and Colonel Tunde Idiagbon were overzealously committed to revamping the economy. They wanted to bring corrupt government officials to book. Indeed most of the major actors under Shagari were tried and found guilty of various offences including corruption. Some of them were sentenced to prison or paid some money as fine.

Unfortunately, in their overzealousness, they became selective in awarding punishment, assumed the toga of fascists and gradually distanced themselves from the sympathy of the people. Unjustifiable and absolutist decrees were enacted like Decrees 4 and 2 of 1984. Against public opinion for mercy Bernard Ogedengbe, Bartholomew Owoh, and Lawal Ojuolape were publicly executed for drug pushing.

On August 27, 1985 General Ibrahim Badmosi Babangida overthrew Buhari. From 1985-May 29, 1999, it was a record of primitive brigandage, absolutist fiat as in the feudal era, terroristic manipulation, and awesome powers of life and death. Those who opposed the power equation were sentenced to death as in Chief M.K.O. Abiola, Kudirat Abiola, Ken Saro-Wiwa, Shehu Yaradua and others whose deaths were concealed.

The death squad of the regime imposed fear and a siege mentality that made life less sweet and monotonous. The opposition was hunted, tortured and detained for a long time without trial.

Corruption became part and parcel of the norms of this ignoble and discredited era. When Babangida first assumed office he appeared to be pro-people and a defender of human rights. But as soon as he got the people's legitimacy and approval, the violence and collective looting of treasury that occurred was rivalled only by General Sani Abacha.

The Nigerian State was privately manipulated; programmes such as the Peoples Bank, the National Directorate of Employment, and the Better Life for Rural Women were some of the pet programmes that were used to siphon huge sums of public money.

By 1987, a transition to civil rule programme was set up and headed by Professor Eme Awa. Sadly, this transition became unnecessarily prolonged. Its assignment was not conclusively carried out in spite of its expenditure of N40b from 1987 - 1993. The need for democratic election became easy alibi for stupendous expenditures.

In 1990, the sum of N100m was given to the two parties created: SDP and NRC for logistic and administrative take off. Government also built the national headquarters of the parties at the cost of N25m each, party offices for the 583 Local Government Areas for about N2.5b, inauguration of National Electoral Committee in 1987 for N16m, building of Party Headquarters for the thirty States N5.3m each, about N10.b was given to the Centre for Democratic Studies headed by Professor Omo Omuruyi, about N400m for the Better Life for Rural Women Programme, the Maryam Babangida Centre built for N1.5b, and Babangida's Third Heritage Home cost about N200m.

According to the Pius Okigbo Panel, the sum of $12.2b (N268b) was siphoned during the Ibrahim Babangida regime. It noted, that money 'went into what could neither be adjudged genuine high priority nor fully regenerative investment.' This it noted 'represent a shameful gross abuse of public trust.'[39]

From 1987 to 1993, corruption became a direct principle of state policy and assumed a monstrous and regrettable magnitude. No project takes place without colossal misapplication of funds. Extra-budgetary expenditure became an officially sanctioned norm. From 1989 it stood at N15.3b, and rose to N59b in 1993.

This amazing and shocking revelation made Nwankwo to declare that;

---

[39] Akani Christian, *Political Economy of Secret Cults in Nigerian Universities* (Port Harcourt, Chriskan Publishers, 1996) P.88.

under him (Babangida) the nation witnessed a perversion of its values, lying became the highest form of statecraft, sycophancy its storm trooper.[41]

General Sani Abacha came at a period when opposition to military dictatorship was at its peak. The country was almost at a brink of collapse and it was self evident that Chief Ernest Shonekan, leader of the Interim National Government was not in control.

In other to stablise, Abacha and his aides, whom he later betrayed and tortured, wooed the civil society and even the human rights groups. As soon as he emerged, his poisonous fangs like those of a jackal gradually manifested. In his maiden address, he stated that "this government is a child of necessity with a strong determination to restore peace and stability to our country and on these foundations, enthrone a lasting and true democracy."

By 1995, he organised a Constitutional Conference with about 96 people nominated by the government. When in August it concluded its assignment, the sum of N5b had gone. Like his predecessor, a transition programme was set up in 1996 and gulped more than N14.2b; party conventions got N600m. It was in one of these conventions that he was nominated as a presidential aspirant. According to Moses Gido;

> Looking at the achievement of the great General in terms of economic stability in which he proved himself a crusader of peace as demonstrated in Sierra Leone and Liberia, a man of prudence and integrity, a man who protects the sovereign integrity of this nation, I nominate him as the presidential candidate of our great party.[42]

As each party struggled to present Abacha as their candidate, a lot of money went into private hands. In 1998, a group known as Youth Earnestly Ask for Abacha (YEAA) under Daniel Kanu was formed. In its so-called two million-man match in Abuja to make Abacha become a life President, it spent the sum of N900m. Musicians were paid some money to

---

[41] Arthur Nwankwo Op. Cit p71.
[42] *This Day* Newspaper Wednesday April 1, 22.

dance and sing Abacha's praises. Abacha Committee of Friends got N2m for peace flag, N35m to produce wrapper with Abacha's name, and the porous vision 2010 conference of 180 members gulped more than N2b.

Members of his family and the Chagouris had a field day. While Abacha's son got a $74m contract for a nation-wide vaccination, his daughter Zainab got another contract of N500m to print voters card for the National Electoral Commission, NECON. The Chagouris had the responsibility of importing fuel when it became scarce in 1996. They made about $20m every month.

Recently, Mohammed Abacha revealed that his father dashed him the sum of $700m. Almost all facets of the economy succumbed to Abacha's corrupt practices. The unconscionable way in which Abacha and his friends looted the economy made Gani Fawehinmi to call him 'a robber'. By June 8, 1998 when he died, the sum of $20b had been fraudulently looted from the nation's account. The family was later made to return the sum of N6,596b.[43]

It may be difficult to document the exact amount stolen by Abacha and his companions. It would appear that;

> Abacha was able to perpetuate one of the most comprehensive plunder and looting of the resources of State in contemporary history through intimidation, brigandry and a plethora[44] of conduits.

As General Abdulsalami Abubakar replaced Abacha, the rotten statuesquo was maintained. He came at a time of national tragedy, torn between peace and war. He, therefore had no alternative than to carry some pretensions of progressive commitment. He appeared physically sober, innocent, gracious and filled with a sense of mission.

This mission rivalled the looting record which his predecessors had set. In line with their tradition, he set up the Independent National Electoral Commission INEC. Within ten

---

[43] Arthur Nwankwo *Op Cit* P. 124.
[44] Ibid P. 125

months INEC had spent about N4b, the National Assembly complex got N15b The Eagle Square prepared by the Julius Berger Company for the May 29, 1999 ceremony got N1.5m. The hosting of the Nigeria '99 N20b, and the National Electric Power Authority got N325m for rehabilitation. All these reduced the foreign reserve from $7b to nearly nothing within ten months. The spending spree became so egregious that it appears no body was in charge. This was why the National Economic Intelligence Committee discovered that about $50m was missing from the nations treasury. According to the *Tempo* Magazine of June 3, 1999, from Babangida's transition to Abubakar, Nigeria lost about N120b.

The Christopher Kolade report noted that Abubakar awarded about 4,072 contracts which amounted to N639.625b.

According to the panel 'this was an embarrassing administrative blunder, totally unacceptable, in a bureaucratic and disciplined establishment'.[45]

In the Nigeria Ports Authority, the sum of N2.4b was used for housing scheme and headquarters. The spending of this money was like a jamboree which 'did not show much prudence'. In the same vein, by the time the Oil Mineral Producing Areas Development Commission (OMPADEC) collapsed in 1996, K. Horsefall had 'spent more than N13, 154.29b between 1992 - 96'.

The result of all these corrupt tendencies, is that corruption has come to be recognised as an official process of property accumulation, small wonder only those who have milked the country dry through their corrupt practices get awards, government appointments and unending titles.

---

[45] *The News* Magazine, 31 April, 2000

Conclusion

Our discussion thus far has shown that the incalculable corruption in the country was made possible because of the control of the state. As soon as a poverty-stricken and hungry looking group grasps state apparatus, wealth accumulation becomes their primary concern. To do otherwise is to be crazy and foolish. The "state itself had become an area for political conflict, rather than an institution capable of standing above and mediating such conflict". It now allocates opportunities and resources.

The result of this is poverty for the people, violence for the society and uncontrollable affluence for the controllers of state power. Budget deficit increased from $761m in 1996 to $1.016b in 1997, external debt in 1995 was $31.93b.

The number of unemployed people increased from 1.3m in 1994 to 4.75m in December, 1995. All these have reinforced thuggery, armed robbery, extreme marginalisation and youth restiveness particularly in the Niger Delta and the Oil bearing areas.

The magnitude of the money stolen by a coterie of unpatriotic Nigerians, especially the military faction of the bourgeoisie from 1996 -1999 made Samuel Aluko to declare that;

> when a nation gives its rule to the military, that nation is finished when a soldier captures a country, what do you expect.[47]

Given the imperialist character and the moral bankruptcy of the Nigerian military, it would therefore be strange to expect any progressive performance from them. Corruption is so much a way of life that evidence of it is thrown about with impunity. Of the 85 countries studied by the Transparency International

---

[47] *Tell* Magazine p.19 April, 15, 2000

in 1998, Nigeria ranked 5th (1.9) in Corruption Perception Index.

In conclusion therefore, to curb the propensity of corruption, the Nigerian state must be free from private manipulation. It must be above selfish and sectional considerations.

The ideals of democracy and rule of law must flourish. The state should not be a respecter of groups or persons. All those who corruptly enriched themselves must necessarily face the law. This is the way to prove the impartiality of the state. The controllers of state power must see themselves within the feelings and visions of the people they have sworn to represent. A situation where the feelings of the people and those of their representatives remain antithetical, is purely undemocratic and could breed corruption.

The above are short-term measures. Corruption cannot be stopped with peripheral, dependent and oil and gas economy. An economy that consumes more of what it does not produce, influenced more by foreign taste and produces nothing, but oiled by 'contractocracy', every person is a general contractor and not a producer.

This neo-colonial scenario must be over-hauled by a patriotic and visionary leadership. A leadership that is ready to make sacrifices, wake the followership out of their slumber and structurally diversify the economy. This would be energy sapping but it would make the country assume the mark of a newly industrialising country.

The above will entail the total confiscation of stinkingly acquired wealth. There should be a hall of disdain for all those who brought the country on its knees as a result of their corrupt acts. Corruption is not a natural component of man. It is a historical creation. Once the historical specificity which incubates it is eliminated, corruption will wither away.

Appendix 1

Corruption in Nigeria Youths Earnestly ask for Abacha 2 Million Man –March 3-4 March 1998

1. Sunny Ade N1m Absent
2. Sunney Okosun N900.000
3. Sir Shina Peter N750,000
4. Onyeka Owenu N900,000
5. Femi Kuti N900,000 absent
6. Salewa Abemi N500,000
7. Pasuming Hordar N400,000
8. Daddy Showkey 250,00.000
9. Chichi of Africa N150,000
10. Falady N300,000
11. Kingsley Lekan N150,000
12. Candy Sea N200.000
13. Stella Monye N300,000
14. Zaki Adzee N250,000
15. Healy child N100,000
16. Dan Opus N100,000
17. Lady Balogun N100,000
18. Evi Edna Ogholi N600,000
19. Bright Chimezie N600,000
20 Valentine 100.000
21. Wasiu Marshal N750,000
22. Christy Igbokwe N1m.
23. Victor Uwaifor N700,000
24. Ras Kimono N650,000
25. Orits Williki N500.000
26. Mike Emela N500,000
27. Babo Fryo N250,000
28. Chris Hanen N250,000
39 Sammy Nayi N250,000
30. Love Idris Abbi N150,000
31 Chikezee Moses N200.000
32. Charlino N300,000
33. Mike Okri N500,000
34. Eunice Mokus N100,000
35 Mike Pam N100,000
36 Peggy Imama N100,000
37. Peace Joseph N100,000
38. Kabari Ashabi N100,000

-Source-*Sunday Punch*, March 15, 1998, P 9 -10

Chapter Four

Corruption and the Challenges of Development in the Niger Delta

Dr. Ekeng A. Anam-Ndu[*]

> ...confidence is every where the parent of despotism-free government is founded in jealousy, and not in confidence; it is jealousy and not confidence which prescribes limited constitutions, to bind down those whom we are obliged to trust with power: that our Constitution has accordingly fixed the limits to which, and no further, our confidence may go...
> *Thomas Jefferson.*

I want to thank the Institute of Academic Freedom in Nigeria (IAFN) for choosing corruption in the Niger Delta as the theme of this conference. Perhaps no other theme would have been more apt than corruption coming as it is on the eve of implementation of the Niger Delta Development Commission, the 13% derivation and increasingly, the restiveness and violence following the growing consciousness of relative deprivation in the Niger Delta. Much as the theme is well focused, I am not for the obvious fact that doing a paper on corruption in the Niger Delta is like attempting an evaluation of the extent of destruction cereals in rat infested sylus that no body is willing to salvage but which everyone is struggling to access. Besides, such a paper if not properly situated runs the risk of localising the phenomenon of corruption as if it is unique to the region or as if Niger Delta peoples are uniquely more corrupt than other Nigerians.

Corruption, like instability is a major recurrent issue of governance in Nigeria. Because of its pervasiveness, scale and sophistication, every regime including the most vicious, has always anchored its emergence and legitimacy on an anti-corruption platform. Yet progressively corruption continues to attain crisis dimension in the sense that each important change or development initiated against it becomes decisive for either the success or failure of the government that initiates the change. It is a paradox that although no regime would want to

---

[*] Centre for Advanced Social Science Port Harcourt.

be seen as a failure, none in post Civil War Nigeria has ever taken anti-corruption measures that could score it a pass-mark. The reason for this is to be sought not in the complex socio-political milieu called Nigeria as has been claimed, but in the fraudulent leadership contraption which Nigeria has always had, and which is always a crisis phenomenon itself.

Thus, an understanding of the phenomenon of corruption in the Niger Delta nay, Nigeria must be situated within the context of the character of the Nigerian state and the location of the Niger Delta within that context. The political elite in the Niger Delta will be characterised in an attempt to understand why, contrary to popular theoretical position, that corruption is an inherent component of development, it is, in the Niger Delta, an instrument of internal colonization and underdevelopment.

The necessity to examine the character of the Nigerian state is borne out of the common observation that corruption was less pervasive in the Regions and at the Federal level in pre Civil War Nigeria. This was because a true Federal form and praxis founded on jealousy not on confidence, inchoate though, was able to check the excesses of public men in their exercise of public power. The coming into the public realm in 1966 of uniformed men either totally uninformed or oblivious of the requirements and working of federalism, enamoured by the sermon of unity and confidence in the Nigerian nation as if it was a thing and not a group of men, not only eroded the democratic foundation of the Nigerian state, but also destroyed the dominant myth that guided political action during the regional days, namely mutual jealousy. For over three decades, Nigerians were subjected to an inarticulate consensus and faith in a contraption that was increasingly being privatised. So pervasive was the consensus that tree planting which, in the fringes of the Sahara desert is a value became a national event even in the Niger Delta where clearing of forests is, of necessity part of development. It was this same inarticulate consensus and confidence in public men that made Nigerians to wear the head of dictator Abacha and that of the wife.

What major change in the Nigerian state led to its development? We need be reminded that the regional oriented approach to decolonisation and development of the Nigerian state in a way was a blessing in the sense that it provided attitudinal base for democratic accommodation of our pluralism. To that extent, regionalism if by it is meant mutual jealousy and distrust, was not antithetical to nation building and the development of democracy: rather it was the ethno-regional imbalance at the centre and the internal colonial relationship in each of the regions that impoverished democratic political practice.

The familiar and precarious hegemonic coalition of Hausa-Fulani – NPC/Igbo – NCNC produced political outcomes that held no future for Eastern and Northern minorities as evidenced by the policy posture of the coalition government during the creation of the Mid-West Region in 1962. Unreflectively announcing the creation of the Region as a punitive measure against Yoruba – AG, Prime Minister Balewa stated:

> The Western Region is the smallest of the Regions in the federation but since the people themselves asked for it to be cut, that is the whole trouble... if I am asked for it to be cut, I will not do it...if a particular region is foolish enough, the Action Group, if they continue in the work of confusion; if they continue to ask us to divide them into bits we shall always see to it that they are broken up into bits...and now that they have learnt their lesson, I think that they will stop their incessant cry that their house is being broken into bits.

A policy posture such as cited, and the rigidity with which it is held has always influenced the political mindset of managers of the Nigerian state to date. That state creation was accepted as a pre-emptive strategy against disintegration while the motivating philosophy behind the idea namely equality of access to power was not, is evidenced by the perfect negation of federal principle through overt and covert centralization, in all aspects of our national political life.

Thus, the creation of states as a means of resolving the regional inbalance, liberate ethnic minorities from the stranglehold of the majorities and liberalise access to political power, in essence, failed to do so. The problem of access to power which was the core issue behind state creation was eclipsed by the disturbances of 1964/65 which eventually smouldered into Civil War. With the coming to power of the military in 1966, itself a reflection of the imbalance, its firm hold on power ever since and its unified mode of operations, the monopoly of access to power has increasingly been consolidated. Over the years, the monopoly has created a cohesive, corporate political elite motivated into action by militant Islamic fundamentalism and the gun. Further, state creation exercises meant to resolve perceived structural contradictions became shrouded, at best, in narrow and selfish calculus of ethno-regional gains and losses or at worst used as a screen to cover domination.

In so far as it affects the Niger Delta states, the creation of states has hardly liberated them from the domination of majority groups. It is a popular argument that the struggle to control oil in the Niger Delta state led to the declaration of Biafra. If this is true, it would equally be valid to argue that the hegemonic coalition of the Hausa-Fulani/Yoruba to keep the country united during the Civil War was also so motivated. It is within this Matrix that one can appreciate the domination of the oil sector both in appointments and contracts by members of these groups. The oil sector aside, capital flight from all the Niger Delta State to Aba and Onitsha has never since been reversed.

So far, I have tried to chart in broad strokes the power configuration in the Nigerian State before and after the creation of states and the Civil War. One factor stands out in bold relief namely, oil as a determinant in the power struggle in Nigeria. It is also at the centre of the crisis at the elite level in the Niger Delta. Needless to add that it provides the resources for corruption not only in the Niger Delta but also in Nigeria as a whole. I shall return to this point presently.

Leadership Crisis in the Niger Delta

Ever since the creation of states in Nigeria, the history of which is incontestably accredited to their pioneers, latter day ruling elite in the Niger Delta States have hardly been able to forge in their states, less so in the region, credible and coherent development oriented policies to guide the pursuit and maximisation of the gains they must derive from the contribution which their region has made to the economy and development of Nigeria. An understanding of this situation can be sought against a background of two opposing forces: the politics and dynamics of patriarchal, hegemonic coalition in Nigeria, and the strong republican tradition among Niger Delta peoples which found expression since the early 1950s. The conservative autocrats who accept the patriarchal hegemony in Nigeria as given have always aligned with hegemonic forces not as equal partners, but as agents of domination. Understandably, they are the ones usually recruited by the military as civilian executives; in so-called democratic regimes, our often too familiar declaratory elections also usually favour them. Given the fraudulent basis of their political recruitment, the scale of corruption involved in their administration is better imagined than described as they have to service their hegemonic masters and their support lines. From superintending the affairs of OMPADEC to officiating as Petroleum minister, incumbents of the Niger Delta origin and majority of them were recruited not necessarily to serve and protect the collective interest of the Niger Delta States, but as a means of controlling the mounting tension in the Niger Delta following the peoples awareness of the ever deepening underdevelopment. That they represented the interest of their hegemonic masters is evidenced by the progressive decay of public utilities in the Niger Delta and the deterioration into violence of relations between oil corporations, their host communities and the government. Interestingly almost all of them recruited to service corruption in a large scale through patronage contracts and outright stealing were removed on charges of corruption. Backed by enormous and fraudulently acquired capital, it is the conservative autocrats in the Niger Delta that dominate the political scene.

There is the second category of elite: the democratic radicals who seek to redefine the location of the minorities in Nigeria's federal praxis. During the brief period of Babangida's two party and the popular but controversial open ballot system, the democratic radicals featured prominently at all levels of election and, indeed, the new system shifted power from the conservatives to the radicals in most of the Niger Delta State.

However, these two categories of elite have always been at war with one another, complexified by communal and private competition for political and economic power. The Ogoni crisis serves to illustrate the depth of disagreement between these two categories of leaders. Indeed, most intra-communal clashes in the Niger Delta over oil related issues are traceable to conflict between the conservative autocrats and the radical democrats. Consequently, the leadership produced in the Niger Delta states is always fractured also along this 'ideological' line. Performance or failure in many a Niger Delta State is therefore not an accident given the milieu of cultured opposition within which governments in the region have had to function.

It is within this context that I see corruption in the Niger Delta and indeed in Nigeria as a formidable obstacle to development. In order to understand the basis of this assertion, we need to examine briefly the complex system of corruption sustained exclusively with revenue from the oil sector. The abrogation of the principle of derivation and the centralized control of oil revenue reached its peak between 1979 and 1999 coinciding with the period when corruption reached a point perhaps never before known in the history of Nigeria. This was the period when "Presidential allocation" known to have amounted to between 180 and 250,000 barrels per day was used to service the support line of Gen. Babangida and Gen. Abacha in their self succession bid. The period between 1975 and 1996 witnessed the creation of the largest number of states and local government areas in the country not in response to systemic pressure for structural differentiation, but largely as a largesse from benevolent dictators sitting on oil revenue. It was within this period (1992) that OMPADEC was established to intervene in the neglect in infrastructural development and decay of existing facilities in the oil producing areas. Later, the PTF established as an interventionist body for the whole country, localised its operational base largely in the Northern states thus beefing up the capital base of oppression of the Niger Delta peoples. A comparative impact assessment of both bodies will establish the fact that they failed to intervene as expected; rather they became conduit pipes through which corrupt deals, and outright stealing of oil money were conducted. Both bodies have been scrapped. Yet a bill establishing a body similar to OMPADEC is about becoming law. Some questions remain: Can the Niger Delta Development Commission (NDDC) as it is called solve the multifaceted problem of social development in the Niger Delta? Is the necessity to establish such a body not an indirect admission that revenue allocation that is not reasonably based on the principle of derivation is unlikely to meet the challenges of development in the areas from where revenue yielding products come? In other words, and in broad national perspective, is the establishment of interventionist organisation like the NDDC a necessary and sufficient alternative to proper re-organisation of our fiscal federalism? These questions cannot be addressed here for want of time.

They are, however, central to the issue of corruption and underdevelopment. They constitute part of the dialectics of domination through the conservative autocrats as agents in the Niger Delta.

To return, it was also within this period that the support of some countries in the Wet African sub-region for what later unfolded as "West African Project" was fraudulently secured through allocation of some 10-30,000 barrels per day of crude oil for refining or for sale at premium to crude traders, Gambia, Ghana, Togo, Benin Republic, Cote d'Ivoire, Guinea, Burkina Faso, Mali and Niger Republic benefited from that corrupt project.

Centralised control of oil revenue by the Federal Government and the ease with which the revenue is derived has led to total dependence by state governments on the Federation Account and, consequently, accounts for irresponsible and corrupt handling of financial matters at all levels of government. Doubtlessly, centralisation serves the private and corrupt interest of the managers of the Nigerian state. The existing legal framework meant to regulate relations between oil corporations and oil producing communities is structured to protect that interest. So far, it has however, proved able to suppress revolution through a curious combination of cooptation and private surplus extraction. It definitely cannot promote stability, peace and development.

The crisis of corruption in Nigeria is part of the crisis of the Nigerian state. It can hardly be solved without addressing the crisis of the Nigerian state. It appears to me that we have to accept the necessity of renegotiating the terms of the federal union including a new fiscal federalism that is based on local ownership and control of resources reminiscent of the regional days.

In terms of fighting corruption, it is clear that much cannot and will not be achieved given the timid way the problem is approached, and the embarrassingly shameful trend in our political engineering in which ex-public officials known to have ruined our treasury for years are now deified.

A word or two may prove useful as a conclusion. No matter how skilled our political engineering and how long it lasts, we should be mindful that no end is fated. While we celebrate our lives through corrupt acquisition of wealth and power, we should be mindful that during revolutionary moments, and we are living in such a moment, the most stable regimes could be unexpectedly demystified by the emergence of alternatives. Impostors, drop-outs and schizophrenics may for now become recognisable models of heroic innocence in the on-going game of remaining permanently in transit, the game we call democracy in Nigeria. We should be mindful that the masses are seeking a destination in a re-born country they can call their own.

Chapter Five

Underdevelopment and Corruption in the Niger Delta

Eskor Yoyo[*]

Introduction

We are very reluctant merely to talk about the mess, the dishonesty, the hypocrisy and the stupidity (or misguidance) that are on stage in Nigeria and the world. The situation calls for an elevating inspiration, a new leadership and massive action in Nigeria and elsewhere. Nevertheless, this occasion gives us the opportunity of briefly bringing basic light to Nigerians and the populations of the world on the much orchestrated topic of corruption. The whole subject is enveloped in a thick smoke, and there are those working hard even to thicken this envelope in order to confer a free ride on the licentious wheel of their hypocrisy.

There is in the air today, as there has been throughout the global history of the past five thousand years, a lot of resentment to hypocrisy about, and misunderstanding of the phenomenon popularly called 'corruption'. The concern is that of the underprivileged who are the victims, the hypocrisy comes from ruling classes; the misunderstanding is practically that of everyone else except a possible few, which is why we are here. Karl Marx and Frederick Engles are two other scholars who could have understood corruption with complete clarity, if they had the information available to us and bothered about the topic.

Since the late 1950s we have been interested in the phenomenon called corruption and have kept a keen eye open for it in all the reports we have read about societies in all parts of the world and in all epochs of human existence. What is presented here has as its background the copious factual reports of archaeologists and prehistorians, anthropologist, objective

---

[*] Presented on special invitation to the Institute of Academic Freedom in Nigeria at Port Harcourt.

and critical social historians, and other social scientists out to tell the truth. We have also had the good fortune over the years of reading and reflecting on the writings of generations of social philosophers, writers from all civilisations who mirror the social practices of their environments, and religious, philosophies and writings which are reactions to social practices in this or that society or epoch.

Our aim is to lay bare the foundation and cause of corruption in human society. It is necessary to send to oblivion the very mistaken notion that corruption is unique either to Nigeria or to the so-called third world. It is necessary to explain scientifically why its scale or intensity can be very great in certain situations. When we know the truth we hope that the truth will free us from the blinkers of both ignorance and hypocrisy.

We can only proceed by way of a number of theses which you will permit us not to elaborate. To elaborate them will require writing a large book. Any student of history, law, philosophy, religion or any social science who is interested in corruption can do his research and elaborate any of the theses.

After this introduction, we define some terms which we shall use, present our theses, and end. It is to avoid the misunderstanding, confusion and distortions due to hypocritical or dishonest scholarship that we feel bound to define a few terms.

Definitions

Corruption

The 1972 edition of Chambers' Twentieth Century Dictionary defines 'corrupt' as "to make putrid; to taint; to debase; to spoil; to destroy the purity of; to pervert; to bribe". Corruption consists of depravity, venality or peculation in playing a social role. The word 'peculation' means to appropriate dishonestly to one's own use, pilfer, or embezzle. In the public discussion of corruption in the state or civil society, the most popular reference of it is to such acts as fraud, embezzlement, falsification, perversion designed to gain some benefits for self or favourites, bribery, and nepotism. The advantage gained from corruption is usually wealth, power or social standing in the conventional snobbish and tainted estimation of class society.

Corruption must be taken along with certain kinds of covering up, diversionary or punitive conduct that go with it, such as theft, lying, falsification, hypocrisy, tyranny and violence to men or property. For instance, suppose bribery or embezzlement has taken place, and someone is promoted, denied promotion, or removed from his job so as to conceal it; or suppose an arson or a murder is committed to obliterate the evidence. Very often ethnic or religious bigotry or inherited hatred is exploited to cover up or excuse corruption. Such ancillary acts cannot be divorced from the direct acts of corruption, such as embezzlement and bribery.

Exploitation

The 1972 edition of Chambers' Twentieth Century Dictionary defines 'exploit' as "to make gain out of or at the expenses of". It defines 'exploitation' as "the act of using for selfish purposes". It follows that social systems, such as ancient slavery, feudalism, capitalism and imperialism, where a class work to enrich another class, are exploitative of those who work.

In such systems the master class make gain out of the servant class. It follows also that a system such as mercantilism or any social system in which the resources of the society, like natural resources, roads and inventions, are used for the benefit of a few, while masses of people remain in poverty and misery are exploitative of those who are deprived. In this case, the favoured enjoy their privileges at the expense of the rest of society who remain poor and miserable. It follows, once again, that since in all social systems based on predatory private property, the private wealth owners use their privileges to pursue their various selfish ends, such systems are exploitative.

In this case, the privileged live by acts of using resources for selfish purposes.

Social surplus

In any society where goods are regularly produced over and above what the actual working people in production require for the sustenance of their lives, a social surplus is produced consisting of this excess. Thus the social surplus is what is produced in addition to productive consumption. The latter, i.e. productive consumption, is the share of output needed to repeat the production process, and this part is made up of what is needed to renew equipment and materials and what is needed for the life sustaining consumption of the actual producers according to the consumption culture of the given society.

The social surplus is often called the economic surplus. It is when this surplus is considered in relation to the division of labour involved in the production process or with reference to the whole society that it is called the social surplus.

All the classes or groups of society, such as peasants, fishermen, artisans, slaves, and wage workers whose labour actually generates the physical national income are called 'working people'. All the other class or groups existing in society, such as landlords, money merchants, slave owners, capitalists and their managerial, administrative and other agents of dominance, are sometimes called 'kept up groups'. They are kept up by appropriating the social surplus.

Slavery

Since we characterise capitalism as modern slavery, the terms 'modern' and the term 'slavery' have to be defined. By 'modern' we mean what belongs to industrial society as a consequence of industrialism. Such a society first came into existence in England in the eighteenth century as the result of the industrial revolution. Thus in every part of the world, an industrial revolution has to take place to produce a modern society.

Slavery is a master-servant form of society in which a class of masters own the means of production and distribution and another class completely divorced from this ownership labour full time as servants to the owners to produce wealth for them. The situation is such that the slaves are obliged to labour full time for the masters in order barely to live.

This definition applies to capitalism as well as to pre-capitalist slavery. The main difference between the latter and the former is that in pre-capitalist slavery, the master owns the servant as his property, whereas in capitalism, the master does not own the person of the servant as his property but through the wage-labour condition possesses the labour power of the slave for full-time use. Even if this situation is modified in corporate capitalism by the wage slaves owning some inconsequential shares by way of savings in an enterprise dominated by those who can be nominated to the board of directors, the basic facts do not change. The real owners of the company, the capitalists, or the masters, are those who own large and dominant shares, are businessmen or financiers rather than workers, and can sit on the board of directors.

We have to draw attention to slave-system nature of capitalism because all the books written by the paid agents of the capitalists, including all their text – books in social science, studiously conceal this fact.

Capitalism

Capitalism is a modern master-servant and exploitative society. It is a new form of slave society in which the means of production and distribution are owned by the masters who use wage slaves that produce or sell commodities for a profit for them, a large part of which they accumulated in a perpetual and competitive tussle to enlarge their wealth and power.

Corresponding to this predatory economic base is a wealth-dominated political system based on the political power of the slave-using class otherwise called the bourgeoisie.

Also corresponding to the predatory economic base is a thoroughly selfish, greedy, covetous, grabbing, philistine, dishonest, callous and inhumane culture. The horrendous slaughter which capitalism has perpetrated along its path in the last three hundred years on all continents bears blood – curdling witness to the barbarity of this system. All bourgeois savants, however, out of dishonesty or hypocrisy purport to see in capitalism simply a harmless trading system.

Suffice it to say that a genuine democracy, freedom, honest governance or humanism is incompatible with capitalism. No system so callous can be compatible with a genuine version of these values.

Socialism

Socialism is a non-predatory modern social system based on the community's or the collective working people's ownership of the means of production and distribution; on the sharing of take-home income according to work; on the abolition of master-servant relationship; and on the abolition of the exploitation of man by man.

Socialism is based on the political power of the working people – in contrast to the political power of various parasites which has characterised so-called civilised human society in the last five thousand or so years. This political power of the working people expressed itself as a new democracy, a people-oriented democracy. Being people-oriented, and providing for the first time under civilization an equal opportunity to all, it is the first genuine effort at modern democracy.

Socialist culture is envisioned as and attempts to be thoroughly humane in focus. It is this kind of system, namely, socialism that several countries in the world are trying to evolve after an anti-feudal, anti-capitalist, anti-imperialist, political, industrial, agrarian and cultural revolution. They are doing so in very difficult conditions caused by internal and external enemies of the people. These are actually or nostalgically attached to five thousand years of predatory, parasitic, irresponsible and inhuman social systems in which the working people have been at best nothing but beasts of burden. The adjectives chosen by us only mildly reflect the ubiquitous evidences of breath-taking anti-people greed, cupidity and barbarism uncovered by historical research.

Theses

Thesis 1

The bourgeoisie drum up corruption in order to divert attention from capitalist exploitation.

Thesis 2

The bourgeoisie give and sustain the false impression that corruption is a matter of individual depravity. Attention is thus drawn away from the social and systematic causes. Such a diversion of attention and such a misreading of corruption also switch attention from the social analysis of corruption and from the only real cure, which is a social revolution involving fundamental political, economic, legal, moral and cultural transformations.

Thesis 3

It is the population of working people, who are the main systems of corruption, that are most resentful of it, while some social critics, reflecting their resentment, are vocal in their criticism of corruption. The bourgeoisie encourage the self-critical anti-corruption furor because none of the campaigners is willing or able to trace it to bourgeois society and the processes of its creation. Such knowledge can come only to one with considerable historical knowledge.

Thesis 4

Corruption is a form of exploitation. It is, in fact, the common grease of the machinery of social parasitism.

Thesis 5

Like other forms of exploitation, corruption is one way of privately appropriating the social surplus – subterranean way.

Thesis 6

Corruption is associated with the power or authority to distribute benefits in an unequal society. Such a power or authority implies options about what to do or not do, whom to favour or not to favour, and how. This discretionary power or authority is, in predatory society, regularly abused.

Thesis 7

Corruption is connected with the rise of private individually-owned property in society.

Thesis 8

A great cause of corruption is the urge to leave much wealth or a favoured position to one's children or to favour relatives with some advantage over others. The individual egotism, property inheritance, and the inheritance of position or the capacity to confer position or other favours are a corrupting factor in society. This is one reason why socialists make education free, frown at individualist greed-engendering private property, and seek to limit private property inheritance.

Thesis 9

All anthropological reports show that primitive communal society, ie. the early hunting, fishing, gathering and simple horticultural societies that were or are communal in social structure and social mores know no corruption unless it is introduced by elements from parasitic society. This introduction is normally resisted as long as the communal system can. Corruption characterises class society, ie. Chiefdoms, states or so-called civilizations.

Thesis 10

What historians and social scientists call 'civilization' began to occur some five thousand years ago. Human society, however, is over one million years old on earth and the society of *homo sapiens* between 25,000 and 40,000 years old. Civilization can be defined as the rise of cultures characterised by specialised professions (typically beginning with priesthood, soldiery, handicraft, trade, and administration), the existence of towns or cities, and the existence of a state or a move towards state formation. Every civilization, according to reports, has been corrupt.

Thesis 11

The fact that long existing primitive communal systems were not and are not corrupt demonstrates that corruption is not natural to man or to human society. However, where corruption becomes a general method of obtaining what parasitic society calls achievement, only a specially inspired few will not be corruptible. This is illustrated by the existence of a microscopic few incorruptible Christian and Buddhist monks in communities of Christian or Buddhist worshipers where both the society and the worshipers are generally corrupt and corruptible.

Thesis 12

As primitive communal societies everywhere lost the freedom of each person, their communal independence, and the security of their communal interdependence, they also lost justice, social integrity and their collective control over any tendency to cheat. Corrupt land - grabbing and feuding chiefs, kings, soldiers, mariners, administrators, conventional priests, merchants, money lenders, magicians, pirates, capitalists, etc. took over from five thousand years ago right up to the contemporary socialist effort to reverse this putrefaction by fundamental social and moral changes.

Thesis 13

Civilization in the last five thousand years has consisted of the appropriation of the social surplus (mainly with the aid of arms) and using them to accumulate private property by a parasitic class living a 'life more abundant' by various methods of predation. In all the civilization, the actual creators of the means of 'life more abundant' are left as down-trodden and savagely suppressed mass of misery, subject to slaughter in masters' wars or otherwise.

Thesis 14

The towns have been the centres of corruption in all epochs and on all continents.

Thesis 15

The widespread trade and use of money characterising towns and civilizations accentuate corruption because the use of money facilitates that transfer of wealth, and money gives a general command over goods and people.

Thesis 16

The more urbanised the society is and the more room there is for predatory activity or predatory living the greater the intensity of corruption.

Thesis 17

Evidence of corruption must be looked for in laws, accounting rules, social history, religious doctrines and injunctions, the literature of an epoch or society, and some types of art such as songs. In this regard Machiavelli's book, the *Prince*, is outstanding for its frankness.

Thesis 18

Like all hitherto-existing civilization (if we exclude the contemporary socialist effort) capitalism has been in all its forms, at all its stages of existence, and ever where it exists, a corrupt and corruption – prone social system.

Thesis 19

Capitalism is exploitative in five major ways. These ways are general infection of the society by selfishness, greed, antagonistic individualism and cupidity intensify the tendency to corruption. The five major exploitative ways of capitalism are the exploitation of the wage or salaried slave in the capitalist market; the exploitation of consumers; the exploitation of the society by the use of its resources to promote the selfish interests of a few; the general predatory drive which the capitalist process imparts to the whole society, compelling all (decision making) actors in the capitalist market to seek so-called 'success', or even survival through one form or other of exploitation; and exploitation by the use of state power and governmental positions in favour of the bourgeois accumulators and other parasitic groups.

Capitalism is a massive inducement to the corruption of the human heart. Which social system in which other people are seen principally as means for the achievement of one's own selfish ends is not going to be stubbornly corrupt?

Thesis 20

The embryonic stage of capitalist accumulation is called primitive (or primary) capitalist accumulation. Capitalism is a system of commodity producing and selling enterprises larger than handicraft enterprises. It requires a large or fairly large capital, and the purchasable labour of miserable people to start.

This initial capitals which is also used to pay the initial wage to modern slaves, is primitive capitalist capital. The process by which this capital is acquired is the process of primitive capitalist accumulation. It consists of many sub-processes. In general, these are predatory internal and external trading; monetisation i.e making and distribution of money; the initiation of accumulating and lending banks; the acquisition of the speculation in real estate; government taxation and the use of government revenue for infrastructural and operational support to capitalist enterprise; peculation which usually involves a large – scale stealing and embezzlement of government revenue and other property; and a heartless exploitation of initiating servile labour. To all this, we must add the sale or lease to capitalists or would-be capitalist of enterprise, already started by the government with public funds. We must add also accumulation out of large state salaries and perquisites and accumulation out of agency service to partnership with and highly remunerated managerial services to foreign enterprises. We must add the process of inflation which transfers liquid income and monetizable assets in a big way from all non-businessmen – including the government to businessmen.

In economics, primitive capitalist accumulation is distinguished from capitalist accumulation out of surplus value. The former is the accumulation of the large capital needed to start a capitalist enterprise. The later is the subsequent capitalist accumulation of capital out of the profits being generated in already established capitalist enterprises through the exploitation of wage labour and ancillary forms of predation. Primitive capitalist accumulation is not a once and for all process. It continues in its various forms after capitalist enterprises have been established, partly as one way of enlarging already invested capital or as a means of launching new capitalist ventures.

Everywhere, in all epochs and whichever the sub-process, primitive capitalist accumulation is a thoroughly corrupt process. Only militaristic empire building and estate accumulation in precapitalist slave – owning, feudal, merchant

– city, etc. civilisations can compare with it in the scale and ubiquity of corruption. Actually when a society is passing through primitive capitalist accumulation, all social mores, responsibilities, institutions, and collective constraints are loosened. Money and the market turn everything into a fluid, and individualism, selfishness, the get-rich-quick mania, and countless methods of perversion putrefy the fluid.

Thesis 21

The ruling endogenous economic process in Third World capitalistic countries since the Second World War has been primitive capitalist accumulation. Only in the so-called Newly Industrialising countries like Mexico, Brazil, Israel, Egypt, South Africa, Singapore, India, Pakistan, Taiwan and South Korea is there considerable indigenous capitalist accumulation out of surplus value. Except for India this is done through dependent industrialization, ie. servants, clients of imperialist transnationals in Western Europe, the United States of America and Japan. This is why all over the Third World corruption is a roaring volcano. So it was in Britain, France, Germany, Italy, Japan, Czarist Russia, the United States of America and elsewhere during their periods of mainly primitive capitalist accumulation from the sixteenth to the late nineteenth century.

Thesis 22

As far as Nigeria is concerned, corrupt primitive capitalist accumulation has an amplitude of freedom and scope due to the death of patriotism, the enormity of the 'free' mineral oil revenue entirely available for grabbing, and the absence of any morally inspiring ideology among the country's crudely bourgeoisified elite.

Thesis 23

All the great religions of the world, Christianity, Islam, Buddhism, Confucianism, Taoism, Hinduism, and

Zoroastrianism, have their origins in corruption and social irresponsibility. They were all reactions to deep seated corruption and were efforts to eradicate it from society. They have failed to eradicate corruption when and where they arose and today. Once conventionalised as organised movements, they themselves sank into corruption. These facts demonstrate the futility of giving pride of place to the religious approach to the problem of corruption.

Thesis 24

Although religion as such cannot eradicate corruption, historical data indicate that it is in periods when they are inspired by some transporting humane ideals, or when their kingdoms and empires are falling apart or on the brink of doing so through corruption, that rulers make efforts beyond phoney noises and window dressing to check corruption. Needless to add that such efforts at best partially stem the tide only for a time. Thus patriotism or ideological inspiration in a government can attenuate corruption, but these influences do not last, and fade away quickly, so long as the society remains predatory.

Thesis 25

Some forms of corruption are more visible than others. The attenuation of more visible forms may leave other forms unaffected or even exploit them and give rise to new forms.

Thesis 26

A law render corruption unnecessary by clothing what corruption seeks to achieve with legality. Instead of the President of the Republic bribing each member of the legislative Assembly piecemeal, individually and clandestinely, he may bribe all of them by giving them entirely undeserved salaries and allowances. If the operation of a government owned facility is characterised by embezzlement or bribery, the government may sell the facility. On the surface, such a sale ends the corruption, but the take-over price may be a give-away one, the selection of the buyer may be such that the vendors for the government have a permanent venal interest in the sale, the citizens in general will lose a valuable public asset which they owned, and users of the facilities of the sale may be ruthlessly exploited through mercenary private pricing and favouritism. A third example is that a law may be passed to legalise private practice which went on in clandestinely and steeped in fraud. A fourth example is that prostitution may be simply legalised instead of being eradicated. Legalisation gives it an apparent clean bill of health. All this is to say that an apparent absence of corruption would not necessarily mean a wholesome let alone an acceptable society.

Thesis 27

Military coups cannot eradicate corruption. Hundreds of coups have happened in the history of the world. Even when the coup makers promise to end corruption as they habitually do when they arrive in office, they end up with the armed forces themselves corrupt and the society hardly less corrupt than before their advent.

Thesis 28

The Profumo, Watergate and other such scandals that hit the headlines from time to time in capitalist countries are merely tips of an iceberg. They show that all capitalist countries are deeply corrupt even though the ubiquity of small-scale corruption varies from place to place. The military-industrial complex in the States of America is an example of subterranean semi-institutionalization of corruption in capitalist countries. Organised crime in capitalist countries swims in corruption. All capitalist cities have a vast underworld of crime served by the attendant corruption. Nevertheless, corruption is more visible in the Third World. This is due at least to some extent to primitive capitalist accumulation, less capacity to police the process of 'making a living' in these countries, and the absence of a class that need not engage anymore in petty debasement in order to dominate or 'forge ahead'.

Thesis 29

Only in a communistic type of society where the opportunity to accumulate private affluence is absent or very limited, where the same education is open to all youths, and where not one can exclusively benefit his own children and his other relatives through a high social position attained by himself by merit – only in such a society can corruption be permanently enfeebled and gradually terminated. This can happen because new aspirations in life will be substituted for greed and covetousness, new mores will evolve, popular controls can be effectively erected so long as the system is a new democracy, and trying to be a 'good parent' or 'good relative' by leaving a handsome property to one's children or through discriminating against others in favour of relatives, cronies and sycophants will end.

Thesis 30

Thesis 29 shows why we have countries that have taken effective initial steps towards socialism, corruption has been, from all reports, much less than in the pre-existing feudal, capitalist, imperialist or semi-colonial regimes.

Thesis 31

The countries building socialism are a minority in a world whose past from 1860 to 1920 was entirely capitalist and whose present is still majority capitalist. Internally and externally the countries building socialism confront bourgeois minded, bourgeois reformist, corrupting and counter-revolutionary opposition. These countries are, therefore, not able to build socialism or a corruption. The socialist inclined communistic system on foundations free from capitalist entanglement and countries are not writing their socialist effort on a clean slate.

This slate will remain a dirty one until in the world as a whole capitalism becomes a small and feeble majority.

Thesis 32

Corruption in the public sector is more prominent because the public is more interested in it, and public attention is focused on it. Hardly anyone takes notice of corruption in the private sector because what the private sector does to 'get on' or 'succeed' is 'private' unless it touches the public sector. When the public sector is corrupt, this indicates that civil society is corrupt. So long as civil society remains selfish, covetous, philistine, grabbing and vilely competitive, it will be corrupt. As long as it is corrupt, incorruptibility in the public sector will remain only a dream.

Thesis 33

As far as the public sector is concerned, the spoils system, associated with the appointment, spending and discretionary powers of president and governor coupled with the lobby system that goes with it is more corruptible than the Westminster system that served Great Britain and the Dominions in the British Commonwealth of Nations for a long time.

Thesis 34

Corruption in the public sector cannot be legitimately used as an argument for the latter's privatization in so far as corruption in the federal, state and local governments in Nigeria, for instance, does not suggest that we should not have governments. The fact that the Babangida and Abacha Presidencies in Nigeria were corrupt does not call for a privatisation of the Nigerian presidency. It does not point up that Nigeria should be governed by a private company so that the Presidency will wind up being the office of the chairman of the Board of Directors of the All-Nigeria Conglomerate of

Private Companies, Limited. The Nigeria Police should then be up for sale to the Police Services Company of Nigeria with unlimited liability.

Thesis 35

Corruption is a non-central issue. The issue to focus on has not changed in the last five thousand years. It was exploitation and what it rests on, namely selfishness, greed, covetousness and the derivative inhumanity. Today the contemporary issue to focus on is capitalist exploitation in all its forms, resting as it does on greed, selfishness, covetousness and the concept of man as a beast of burden or a slave to man. Corruption is a red herring; it is diversionary.

Conclusion

We came not to debate but to draw attention to the important but little known facts in order to settle accounts with ignorance, misguidance and hypocrisy.

The literature that gives evidence on corruption is like the sea. Let the interested reader begin to search, starting, if possible, with histories of civilization. We refrain from drawing attention to any set of writings, lest a reader be turned away from his own search, believing that without that particular set of writings he is handicapped. The present paper is served as a trigger.

Appendix 2

Conference evaluation

S/N	Questions	Excellent	Good	Fair
1	Provision of information before the Conference	3	7	3
2	Access to Venue	4	8	1
3	Arrangements for Conference Registration	8	5	-
4	The way the Conference was structured	6	6	1
5	The way Presentations and discussions were conducted	6	10	1
6	The Venue and refreshment	2	4	3
	Total	29	40	9

Most participants felt that access to the venue was good and the provision of information before the conference was also good. The registration for the conference on the whole was seen to be excellent. Participants found that the structure of the seminar was very good and that discussions were well conducted.

Most participants also felt that the majority of the speakers were very good, and presentation informative. At the same time, some participants were concerned that their time was not enough for general discussion.

The most important aspect of the conference was the opportunity the participants had to meet new people and network. The information gained from the seminar including access to documentation was seen to be very important.

Few participants felt that there was an aspect of the conference that was less important. Those that did, however, felt that the irrelevance or propaganda of government agencies was unhelpful. Participants in general were very pleased with the conference and many of them thanked IAFN staff and USAID/OTI for their hard work. They also expressed a wish to have the follow-up report on the conference made available to them.

List of Participants

S/N	Name	Organisation	Address
1	Gloden Reuben	Institute of Human Rights	RTA Industrial Layout
2	Eme Ndeh	Women in Nigeria (WIN)	106 Ikot ekpene road, Uyo, Akwa Ibom
3	Wellington Itam	The Tide Newspaper, Legal Advice Centre Aba	4 Ikwerre road, Port Harcourt, 80A Ohanku Rd. Aba
4	Saviour O Akpan Esq	State Ministry of Information	State Secretary Complex Port Harcourt.
5	Lucy Nna-Weli	FIDA Rivers State	No 121 Victoria St. PH
6	Olima Obene (Mrs.)	FIDA, Rivers	121, Victoria Street, PH
7	Castn Dangudi	The P.H. Telegraph	NUJ Moscow Rd P.H.
8	Emmanuel Osarokio	The Guardian Newspaper	24 Ikwerre Road, Port Harcourt
9	Ndidi Orulu	Mosop	Port Harcourt
10	Meneh Gabarabe	South-South express	8 Bishop Dimiari St. GRA PH
11	Ben Adoga	South-South	8 Bishop Dimiari St. GRA PH
12	Odudu Okpongate	WIN Rivers State	13 Agudama St. D/line P.H
13	Emem J. Okon	Community Rights Initiative (CORI)	29 Ikwerre Road, port Harcourt
14	Chizor Wisdom Dike	The PH Relegraph	NUT, Moscow Road
15	Mrs. Joy Duncan	Rivers State Judiciary	16 Harbour Road
16	His worship M. O. Chukwu	Rivers State Judiciary	8 Harbour Road
17	Churchill Ibeneche Esq	C3RJ	3 Ozuzu Close PH
18	Nelson Azibaolanari	MORETO	Ogbia
19	Com. Napoleon H. Ewoh	NLC	Ahoada East
20	Wodi Godwill	PILL	1A Wodi New Layout

	Chinweikpe		Elelenwo
21	Dr. Akaninwo	Bio-Chemistry Dept.	Uniport
22	Dr. Patrick Achibong	USAID/OTI	No 31 Apara Road. GRA
23	Rev. Mrs. I. O Efion	Centre for Training and Gender Activities	5A Archibong Eso Lane, Calabar
24	Dr.N.E. Bassey Duke	Congress for Democracy, Transparency and Good Governance	45 Akim Road, Calabar
25	Isu Menidin Azibola	ND-HERO	Blaock 3B Federal Road
26	Charity Eke-Jilam	NTA Port Harcourt	Choba Road, Uniport
27	Ayasuk, Temple E	Centre for Responsive Politics	12 pots Johnson St. PH
28	Harry I.	Personal	RSLB, PH
29	Erekosima A.	IHRHL	Port Harcourt
30	Chris Jonah	C.D	BL B. 137 R. Barracks Port Harcourt
31	Patterson Ogon	ICHR	13 Agudama Ave. PH
32	Prof. Eskor Toyo	Dept. of Economics	University of Calabar
33	Joe Inyang	Youths Rights Action Network (YORAN)	13 Aguadama Ave. Port Harcourt
34	Obodoekwe Steve	CLO Rivers State	13 Agudama Ave. Port Harcourt
35	Dr. Ekeng A. Anam-Ndu	CASS	13 William Jumbo Street, Port Harcourt.
36	Patrick Bassey	Development Action Programme	26A Eyo Edem Street Calabar.
37	Roibito Ekpiken Ekanem	USAID/OTI	31 Apara Road, GRA Phase II, Port Harcourt
38	Chima Boms, Esq	Boms & Boms (SUPABOAD), Second floor	No, 1 Azikiwe road, 234643
39	Onyike I. Osoka	Historical Society of Nigeria	University of Port Harcourt
40	Ruskin Amadi	Community News Newspaper	No 7 Rumuola Road, Rumuokwuta, Port Harcourt
41	Chidi Wosu	WIN Rivers State	Apani
42	ChiChi Akara	Radio Rivers	Port Harcourt

43	John Bibor	Journalist	Port Harcourt
44	Sunny Anya	CDHR	Port Harcourt
45	Cletus Ugbana	CDHR	Port Harcourt
46	Richard Ihunwo	ISC	Port Harcourt

Programme

Venue: Royal Garden Hotel, Rumuomasi, Port Harcourt
Time: 10 a.m
Date: 26th – 27th May 2000

Day 1
First Session   11.30 am – 1.30 pm
1. Topic   **Political Economy of Corruption in**
                  Nigeria
                  Dr. A. A. Nwankwo
                  Chancellor
                  Eastern Mandate Union

2. Topic   **The Nigerian State as an Instrument of**
                  Corruption
                  Akani Christian
                  Executive Director
                  Institute of Academic Freedom in Nigeria
                  (IAFN)
                  Questions/Comments

Chairman of Session
O.C.J. Okocha. SAN, JP
Manuchim Chambers
Part Harcourt

                  Lunch break
Second Session   2pm – 3.30pm
1. Topic   **Corruption in the Niger Delta:**
                  Challenges of Development
                  Dr. Ekang Anam Ndu
                  Director of Operations
                  Centre for Advanced Social Science (CASS) –
                  Port Harcourt
2. Topic   **Underdevelopment and Corruption in**
                  the Niger Delta
                  Professor Esko Toyo

Department of Economics
University of Calabar
Questions/Comments

3. Working Group/Discussions

Chairman of Session
Dr. Gabriel Okara
Port Harcourt

First Session
1. Topic   **Militarism and Corruption in Nigeria**
                Dr. Eme Ndu
                Department of Political Science
                University of Port Harcourt

2. Topic   **Nigerian Law and Corruption**
                Chief S. I. Okogbule
                Faculty of Law
                University of Science and Technology
                Nkpolu, Port Harcourt.

                Questions/Comments

3. Working Group/discussions

Chairman of Session
Dr. Mrs. Akaninwo
Biochemistry Department
University of Port Harcourt

Communique

Vote of thanks by – Nimi David West Director Women Affairs
                IAFN

Index

West African Project, 61
Western Liberal Perspective, 9, 10
Westminster system, 80
Wheeler- Dealers, 22
White Elephant Projects, 43
World Bank, 3,5
World Scout Jamboree, 43

Y

Yinusa Paiko (Alhaji), 44
   -panel, 44
Yoruba, 57, 58
   - race, 28
Youth Earnestly Ask for Abacha (YEAA), 49

Z

Zambia Anti-Corruption Commission, 5
Zarie (Congo), 2
Zimbabwe, 3,
Zoroastrianism, 76

www.ingramcontent.com/pod-product-compliance
Lightning Source LLC
Chambersburg PA
CBHW021836020426
42334CB00014B/650